The
PERFECT INSULT
for Every Occasion

A. C. Kemp
"Lady Arabella Snark"

Aadamsmedia
Avon, Massachusetts

Copyright © 2008 by A. C. Kemp
All rights reserved.

Published by Adams Media, an F+W Publications Company
57 Littlefield Street, Avon, MA 02322. U.S.A.
www.adamsmedia.com

ISBN-13: 978-1-59869-327-0
ISBN-10: 1-59869-327-1
Printed in the United States of America.

J I H G F E D C B A

**Library of Congress Cataloging-in-Publication Data
is available from the publisher.**

The world of Lady Arabella Snark is entirely fictional. Names, characters, places, and incidents either are the product of the author's imagination or are used fictitiously, and any resemblance to actual persons, living or dead, business establishments, events, or locales is entirely coincidental.

This publication is designed to provide accurate and authoritative information with regard to the subject matter covered. It is sold with the understanding that the publisher is not engaged in rendering legal, accounting, or other professional advice. If legal advice or other expert assistance is required, the services of a competent professional person should be sought.

—From a *Declaration of Principles* jointly adopted by a Committee of the American Bar Association and a Committee of Publishers and Associations

Many of the designations used by manufacturers and sellers to distinguish their product are claimed as trademarks. Where those designations appear in this book and Adams Media was aware of a trademark claim, the designations have been printed with initial capital letters.

*This book is available at quantity discounts for bulk purchases.
For information, please call 1-800-289-0963.*

This book is dedicated to the memory of Baroness Eloise Bosquet de Wagner Wehrborn, whose pioneering work in the field of etiquette has been an inspiration.

Contents

"If you haven't got anything nice to say about anybody, come sit next to me."

—Alice Roosevelt Longworth

one. Common Discourtesy

In which we meet LADY SNARK, ETIQUETTE GURU & former director of the Haverford Women's Correctional Facility CHARM SCHOOL FOR REPEAT OFFENDERS, who explains, among other things, the most unusual manner of her husband's DEATH, the reason that SHAKESPEAREAN INSULTS might not be the most WOUNDING SLIGHTS to use against the English professor you were sleeping with to get a better grade, & the meaning of a SPANISH OBSCENITY.

Lady Snark Deigns to Write a Letter Explaining Why She Is Going to Help You, Even Though You Probably Do Not Deserve It

My Dears,

Since my conditional release from the Haverford Women's Correctional Facility earlier this year, I have been overwhelmed with pathetic letters asking for my assistance. Apparently, most people are helpless in the face of smarmy coworkers, obstreperous children, and elderly relatives who refuse to die. Nor do they have any idea what to do when they find their husband in a conjugal embrace with the burly gardener in the potting shed or discover that their parking spot at the country club has been taken over by the titanic vehicle of a gangsta rapper.

If you are unfamiliar with my reputation, you may wonder why so many unfortunates are lining up for my pearls of wisdom. Allow me to explain how I came to be a guru of etiquette, interpersonal relationships, and alternative uses for fireplace pokers.

The Haverford Women's Correctional Facility Charm School for Repeat Offenders

While serving time for the death of my husband, Lord Snark (though I had nothing to do with that crocodile and have no idea how it found its way into his bathtub), I was told I was required to perform some sort of "service" at the prison. With options like cleaning the toilets or working in the kitchen (which would have forced me to see firsthand what went into the food we were expected to eat) I thought it would be better to create my own job and suggested a class in deportment.

I suppose the fact that I was incarcerated at the time might give you a false impression of my standing, but I have lived among the upper echelons of society for most of my adult life (with the exception of that brief, unhappy sojourn on the cannibal island). I am therefore well versed in the social graces and, for one wretched year, I even imparted my wisdom to impressionable young girls at the Lizée boarding school in Fall River, Massachusetts.

The prisoners' class started out traditionally enough. Students practiced elocution and posture, and studied the finer points of genteel conduct, such as when it is appropriate to steal someone's jewelry and what kind of stationery is best for blackmail notes.

But for all that I tried to provide a well-rounded education on all matters related to good manners, the inmates' questions tended to focus on dealing with people they did not care for, such as those who had criticized their cell decoration or looked at them the wrong way in the cafeteria line. Indeed, the majority of the questions I was asked were different manifestations of the same eternal riddle:

How can I deal with annoying persons in a way that utterly crushes them without tarnishing my carefully developed reputation or extending my already lengthy prison sentence?

How I Came to Write This Book, Which I Hope Will Be a Ray of Sunshine in Your Otherwise Dreary Little Life

I soon discovered that though the particulars might differ depending on one's situation, this was a question that troubled many people. Only a few weeks after our cozy discussion group began, the girls were so beguiled with my advice that they began to bring me requests for help from their friends and families far outside the electrified fence of our residence.

At first I demurred, mentioning to my cellmate Tabitha that, as entertaining as it is to tell people what to do, I was not getting any remuneration for the task and could better spend the time inventing pleading letters (ostensibly from my servants) appealing to the governor to shorten my sentence.

Quickly sizing up the situation, she suggested requesting a small donation for each letter I answered. This proved an excellent solution; soon our cell was replete with lavender sachets, down coverlets, high-end vodka, some nice mid-century English lithographs, and a large boombox that played the song "Caribbean Queen" in an endless loop. (The last being Tabitha's request, I am not sure if its monotonous offerings were by accident or design. She seemed to enjoy it.)

Over the next few months, I answered an increasing number of letters from persons at every level of society until I could scarcely keep up with the demand; my reputation for excellent advice on manners spread with the speed and reach of an infectious disease until I felt I was the very Typhoid Mary of etiquette.

Foe or Faux?

Test your knowledge of vituperation by determining if the following is an insult or not.

Caleb, your philodendron is the most etiolated houseplant I've ever seen! How did you do it?

This is an insult. Caleb's greenery is a pale, spindly shadow of its former self, most likely because it did not receive enough sunlight.

When my attorney, Marcus de Frise, became aware of the lucrative potential for my brilliant insights into the human condition, he suggested expanding my efforts and using the proceeds to defray the ever-increasing costs of maintaining my innumerable residences while incarcerated. Marcus and Tabitha think alike; if she were not serving five consecutive life sentences for that little mixup with the armored car, I think they would make an ideal couple.

Given the tremendous success of my "consulting" business, along with a few potentially damaging personal photos of publishers that had come into my possession, Marcus managed to secure a book contract for me, the result of which you now hold in your hands.

It is my heartfelt wish that this book will change your life for the better. If you find it does, feel free to send a note to Judge Oberlus Ouellette at the courthouse in Augusta to let him know how much happier you are for having read it. I am hoping to improve the somewhat unfavorable impression he has of my character based on some information that has recently come to light regarding the death of an earlier spouse.

Cordially,

Lady Arabella Snark

Elfingrot Manor
Bar Harbor, Maine

How to Crush Annoying Persons: An Overview

While the number of social altercations you may find yourself in is limitless, there are only two hard and fast rules for coping with them. First, you must consider whether your unkind words have the potential to boomerang and result in something untoward, such as permanent disfigurement, unemployment, or an irate waiter's very unsavory addition to your crème brûlée.

Second, assuming you wish to spew a truly destructive torrent of oral lava, you must take your adversary's background and educational level into account and speak in terms most likely to burn down his or her psychological village. Let's take a look at a hypothetical example in order to examine these rules in more detail.

Trail of Tears: Symbolic Handkerchiefs in the Later Novels of Thomas Hardy

Your grades have just come in the mail and Chad, your English 101 professor, has given you a D. This comes as a surprise to you because you have just spent the last fifteen weeks sleeping with Chad for the very purpose of avoiding that outcome.

At first, you think this is a mistake, but Chad now refuses to take your phone calls and it is becoming apparent that he has played you. As a result, you decide that you will pay him a visit to express your feelings.

It may be difficult to find him if your previous meetings have all taken place in the classroom and Room 6 at the Dew Drop Inn. Chad is not a real professor, but only an adjunct who works part time at four universities, none of which give him health benefits. Thus, instead of trading philosophical witticisms at the expense of Derrida with senior faculty over sherry in an oak-paneled library, he spends most of his time in a converted janitor's closet with three equally degraded officemates, reading through the incoherent ramblings of undergraduates like you while breathing in toxic mold and leftover cleaning solution.

Now you are at the door of his office and for the purposes of this exercise, you may assume that he is not alone; Dean Sanchez was walking by when she noticed a light from the closet and stopped out of curiosity to see what was going on inside. Let us examine six possible remarks that may have occurred to you on your way here from the dorm and analyze each for style and effectiveness. Given your level of scholarship, I apologize in advance if this section's resemblance to a multiple-choice quiz makes you break out in hives.

Number 1. **I hope you die, crudball!**

This is certainly appropriate for your social status as a college student; no one would think less of you for being direct. However, in this situation, it will not work. English instructors hear this insult so often when grades come out that it barely registers.

Number 2. **Marble-hearted fiend! Most villainous knave! Spotted snake with double tongue!**

This has the benefit of taking your audience into account. Even though his specialization was the Naturalist Movement 250 years later, Chad will know these insults are Shakespearean. He may not hear them as insults, however. That's because what you are really saying is, "Here are some erudite hostilities that I trust you to recognize and understand based on your massive intelligence and comprehensive liberal arts education."

For this reason, Chad will not be thinking about the meaning of these venomous quotes; rather his brain will be whirring as he tries to remember which plays they came from. "*Lear*! *Othello*! And the last one is . . . uh . . . *A Midsummer Night's Dream*! Ha!! How clever I am." Note that, up to this point, I have been too polite to mention that if you had remembered any of those quotations for the final, you would not be in this situation.

Number 3. Me cago en la leche que mamaste.

How canny of you to think of this incredibly base insult from your semester abroad in high school. And why am I not surprised that all the Spanish you remember from that learning experience is an insult that means "I defecate on the milk that you sucked from your mother's breast"? Alas, you have misjudged your audience. Chad does not speak Spanish, unlike Dean Sanchez.

Number 4. The length of your dissertation title is inversely proportionate to the size of your manhood!

This is much closer to the mark; the title of Chad's dissertation was "Trail of Tears: Symbolic Handkerchiefs in the Later Novels of

Thomas Hardy, Including an Analysis of Meaningful Monograms and Floral Patterns." He is also still smarting that no one wanted to publish it. However, you might not want to say this in front of the dean, as the rules that exact severe punishment on Chad for sleeping with you also exact severe punishment on you for sleeping with Chad.

Number 5. **How would you like it if I hit you over the head with this heavily annotated version of the** *Canterbury Tales,* **edited by Zoë Michaels-Zenworth and Elmira Bitterson Lourdes (2nd edition, 1984) until you bleed from your ears?**

....

This statement contains several egregious mistakes. First, you should never announce that you are going to attack someone. Chad will have already gone for his unabridged dictionary in defense. More importantly, you should never resort to violence without extensive planning if you do not wish to be caught. Finally, this will not satisfy your goal, whether it is raising your G.P.A. or lowering Chad into a six-foot hole. No one has ever died from scatological humor, no matter how heavy.

Number 6. **Chad, I just wanted to tell you how much I learned from your class. I'm planning to post something on the anonymous *professorank.com*, but I wanted to let you know first, so you could go and look at what I had to say about it. Thanks so much for teaching me the true meaning of scholarship!**

If you are paying attention, you will have noticed that the vague wording of the apparent compliment in remark number six is actually a veiled threat, making it the best answer. Hopefully, Chad will read between the lines and see that what you are really going to post will be something like "Chad's class wasn't very interesting, but he was one of the best customers for my meth lab." This approach, while less linguistically satisfying than a foreign or literary insult, might result in your passing the class as Chad suddenly discovers an error in his grade calculations.

Prepare Now to Dive into the Sea of Enmity, in Which You Have Heretofore Only Dipped Your Toe

Now that you have some sense of how getting the upper hand works, it is time to begin looking at the specialized approaches and vocabulary that you will need to deal with particular persons, places, and situations. From holy rollers and the grammar police to troublesome party guests and playground bullies, I will show you the best way to assert your dominance and shred all those who stand in your way, until even the most imposing redwood of a foe is naught but innocuous mulch. In this manner, not only will you improve your interpersonal relationships, but you will also save money on landscaping.

two. A Fork in the Eye: Persons Who Erroneously Believe Themselves to Be Better than You

In which we consider ETERNAL DAMNATION; learn how to puncture the inflated egos of CONDESCENDING BOORS; revisit the importance of GRAMMAR, GREEK, and LATIN; & explore the various moral reasons that one should not send one's children to a SWISS BOARDING SCHOOL.

The Unbearable Superiority of Being

Helène Hébert, who lives downstairs from my Paris penthouse, is forever telling me that if she were me, she would send my stepdaughter Amelia to finishing school in Switzerland to make her more "feminine" so that some nice young man would take her off my hands. Helène, it should be noted, sent her own daughter Solange to the École Promiscueuse in Gstaad, where she apparently learned that femininity is best expressed by dressing like a streetwalker and injecting collagen into your lips until you resemble a largemouth bass. Even Amelia's brother Eric, who has the common sense of a cement block, is afraid of contracting a disease from Solange.

Foe or Faux?

Test your knowledge of vituperation by determining if the following is an insult or not.

Oh, Madge! Whenever I think about you and that little problem with your husband, I can't help but feel a great deal of schadenfreude.

This is an insult. The speaker is taking immense pleasure in Madge's misfortune.

I mention my Gallic neighbor because she is a representative of an alliance of people whom, if the world were flat, I would push off the edge. This association also includes those who "correct" my pronunciation of *tomato* and *neither*; those who claim to be above watching television, yet have an encyclopedic knowledge of the programs they are too exalted to see; and those who think I am damned to eternal hellfire because I refuse to renounce my sins publicly in an indoor swimming pool wearing nothing but a transparent muumuu.

Suffice it to say that Helène and her cartel of condescension are no match for me. Over the years, I have mastered a number of effective responses to such noxious remarks.

When I was a slip of a girl, for example, I traveled to Paris on a steamer in the company of Nick, a seemingly worldly poet I had met at the automat. When you are sixteen, there is something dangerously appealing about a man who stands with a cigarette dangling slackly from his lower lip, an attraction which disappears only after the hot ash thereof has fallen on your bare foot.

Nick and his equally annoying beret-encrusted friends made it clear that my convent school education in Bismarck was "not quite the thing," even as they swilled *les bières* purchased with the sweat of my work as an artist's model. They felt that to be a true sophisticate, you had to have been born in a densely populated area near a large body of water and were unimpressed by my observation that lemmings would fit that description.

After a week, I left Nick to buy his own beer and didn't see him again until twenty-three years later, when he was modeling a men's corset on the Sri Lankan twenty-four-hour shop-from-home channel. This demonstrates the first method in protecting yourself: You can simply remove yourself from the source of the toxic emissions.

As a secondary technique, physical violence can be quite effective when dealing with snobs. For this reason, I have always allowed Amelia to accompany Solange when she goes out "clubbing." However, I have recently learned that clubbing in Paris now refers to dancing, drinking, illicit drugs, and indiscriminate sexual encounters—it has nothing to do with baby seals or responding to inappropriate taunts in the ladies' room.

While somewhat less satisfying than pummeling your attacker's head into the shape of a pancake, I have been told that words can also be used for the purpose of defending oneself against would-be critics, and, in the opinion of my parole officer, they are the superior means. Therefore, words are what we will focus on in this chapter.

Hell in a Handbasket: Pathetic Laments of the Grammar Police

Dear Lady Snark,

Is it appropriate for me to correct another guest's grammar when at a social gathering? My girlfriend says it's not, but it's so irritating! Listening to people split infinitives or use *that* when they mean *which* is just like fingernails on a chalkboard. Please tell her it's okay for me to set these morons straight so that my beloved language will not continue its downward spiral into the toilet.

Kevin

Short Hills, New Jersey

My Dear,

Is it appropriate? Well, yes, if you want to look like a dweeb. There are worse sins than to unintentionally (or intentionally) split an infinitive,

Kevin. Personally, I find clichés like "fingernails on a chalkboard" rather irritating, and yet I do not plan to visit your home and end my suffering with a pillow over your face while you sleep, even though I know where you live by your return address.

Tase-tee Whore-dee-vors

At cocktail parties, for example, one sometimes meets those whose ability to string together words into a meaningful utterance is mildly impaired, as shown below.

> **Jeff: Oooh-wee! Them grayer cheese whore-dee-vors is damn good tase-tee! You want try?**

Though you might gain some satisfaction from pretending otherwise, you have no trouble deducing the import of Jeff's invitation. He means to say "Oh, my! The Gruyère hors d'oeuvres are exceptionally delicious. Would you care for one?"

As much as this flouting of verbal convention might grate on your nerves, there is no point in correcting him. Jeff will neither understand your correction nor your motivation for informing him of his verbal "blunder." If you honestly believe that anyone questions your erudition compared to Jeff's, go ahead and say something for the benefit of the other guests. Otherwise, just take a "tase-tee whore-dee-vor" and move on.

Foe or Faux?

Test your knowledge of vituperation by determining if the following is an insult or not.

My, what Brobdingnagian feet you have, Clarice!

This is an insult. Clarice's feet are enormous, like the giants in Gulliver's Travels.

The Effects of Opiates on Grammar

"But!" you cry out, "There are situations in which people are horribly ungrammatical and I must correct them for the sake of upholding certain standards."

Perhaps. However, situations in which native speakers use truly ungrammatical sentences generally occur only when said speaker is heavily drugged or brain damaged and are therefore rare (unless you have established an opium den in your guest room, in which case you might encounter them more often).

The kind of "ungrammatical" sentences you mean, I suspect, are those in which the speaker's grammar is still comprehensible, but adheres to the rules of a nonstandard dialect. For example: "Ha, ha! You ain't got no hair! Your too-pay done fell off."

The linguistic term for this is *annoying*. Note that the superior feeling you might get by comparing the speaker's lower social status to yours in no way mitigates the discomfort brought on by this statement if your toupee has actually fallen off.

The only time you should really worry about grammar is when your own is questioned by the kind of person who lives for a misplaced adverb so that he or she may roll his or her eyes and sigh knowingly before launching into an impromptu lecture over the canapé tray.

I suspect that you, Kevin, are one of these people. Based on your letter, I imagine you become ecstatic at the possibility of explaining to your ill-fated coworkers why they shouldn't end a sentence with a preposition (while secretly hoping they will provide you with more teaching opportunities by continuing to do so). You need to recognize that resisting all of the "cataclysmic" changes the language has undergone since Thackeray was penning smut in the 1840s is futile. If it makes you feel like a member of a special club, it does: the club of people to whom modern English is unintelligible.

I am not sure that you really want to hear what I am about to say. However, for the benefit of the more linguistically (and socially) secure, like your unfortunate girlfriend, I will now discuss the many reasons you should refrain from appointing yourself the Sultan of the Subjunctive.

The Unhappy Side Effects of Correcting Other People's Grammar, Not Least of Which Is That No One Will Like You

One serious issue is that you will often miss the more important meaning of what someone is trying to tell you. In the following dialogue, grammar "maven" Orville is standing alone (Surprise!) at a party when he is approached by his soon-to-be-estranged wife Annabeth and her lover, Stan.

Stan: Hopefully, it won't be too hard on you when your wife Annabeth leaves you tomorrow and moves in with me.

Orville: Hopefully? What you really want to say is, "I hope," don't you? Because as anyone with a really decent education— you remember that I spent my junior year at Oxford?—as I was saying, anyone worth his intellectual salt knows that *hopefully* is an adverb that should only be used to modify—

Orville does have old-fashioned tradition on his side, but over the last century, a tsunami of "incorrect" usage has essentially destroyed the beach of grammatical righteousness he was standing on (unlike the destruction of his marriage, which would appear to be his sole responsibility).

Foe or Faux?

Test your knowledge of vituperation by determining if the following is an insult or not.

This essay has more otiose language than anything I have ever read.

This is an insult. The essay is full of words that have no value or function.

In a more flagrant example of disregard for both grammar and personal safety, I offer this next example. Elihou has dashed into the quick checkout line at Betty's Food Basket when Enoch notices he has fifteen items.

> **Enoch:** Whoa, bub. This line is for twelve items or less.
>
> **Elihou:** You mean *fewer*?
>
> **Enoch:** Yeah, of your teeth, asshole!
>
> **Elihou:** Aaaah! Stop it!

Yes, you should use *fewer* with nouns that can be counted (like **teeth**) but again, there are many reasons not to question what people are saying to you if it is comprehensible. Looking foolish is only one. In this case, Elihou could have avoided costly cosmetic dentistry by being a little more tolerant. Here are a few more examples of how being a "grammar purist" can get you into trouble.

Negation omissions:

Alex: It isn't "I could care less." It's "I couldn't care less."

Cynthia: Either way, I'm not impressed that your car can parallel park itself. If you've got that much money, put in a driveway.

Modal misuse:

Harriet: If you say "Can I help you?" you're talking about ability. The correct question for a salesperson is "May I help you?"

Sheila: Get out of my store or I may knock you to the ground. I know I can.

Redundancy:

Phil: Lance, come here! You need to move your car before it's completely destroyed by the bulldozer.

Lance: You mean as opposed to partially destroyed? God, I hate it when people butcher English like—(CRUNCH!!)

New word coinage:

Armand: "Deplane"? Are you serious? If you want me to exit the aircraft, why don't you ask me properly by saying—

Flight attendant: Security!

But at least these annoying know-it-alls have the tenuous support of some style guides. Far worse are those who endanger themselves needlessly by correcting people who are not misusing the language, even according to the antiquated dictates of your seventh-grade grammar teacher. These people deserve to die.

The problem here is that the senses are an exception in the adjective/adverb modification rule. To feel bad is to have an unpleasant emotion. To feel badly is to have difficulty sensing things by touch. Sam clearly means the first, while Matilda is an insensitive cow.

Finally, there are few instances of smug-but-wrong language policing as pervasive as the subject-object pronoun error:

> **Ethel:** I'm sorry about the way things turned out, Xaviar. Since Dad left the estate to Michael and me and cut you out of the will, I think it's only fair to share some of—
>
> **Xaviar:** "Michael and I."

Ethel: What?

Xaviar: Dad left the estate to "Michael and I."

Ethel: Xaviar, you have a copy of the will right there. Dad didn't leave you anything because of the whole thing with the country club president's daughter in the boathouse and—

Xaviar: I'm trying to correct you. It should be "I."

Ethel: Well, too bad for you, but you made your bed and I guess you have to lie in it. And don't bother coming to Connecticut for Christmas this year—we'll be at our new house in Aruba.

Xaviar has made two fatal errors: First, he failed to recognize that "me" is quite correct as the indirect object of the sentence. Second, he failed to recognize that if he hadn't been such a jerk, Ethel would have shared her inheritance with him.

I hope this has been instructive, and please know now that if you ever feel compelled to correct my grammar, Kevin, I will stick a fork in your eye.

Cordially,

Lady Arabella Snark

Is That a Plank in Your Eye or Are You Just Happy to See My Mote?

Dear Lady Snark,

When I went to visit my sister last summer, she forced me to go to a tent revival. You may not be familiar with this kind of event—I sure wasn't—but it's a religious meeting in a tent where you have to listen to sermons for days and say "Amen" a lot while fanning yourself against the heat. I'm not particularly religious and I felt really uncomfortable, especially when this strange woman with unnaturally red hair came up to me and said, "Repent now! Pride goeth before a fall!" I had only been talking about my daughter's success in her school spelling bee. How do you respond to something like that?

Geraldine

Black Mountain, North Carolina

My Dear,

How about, "Back off, peaches! The flames of hellfire wafting off your dye-job are singeing my eyebrows"? I am more conversant than you might think in this area; the first time I was incarcerated, the prison chaplain developed an unhealthy interest in my eternal soul and all the worldly flesh that surrounded it. Consequently, I know the Good Book well enough to see that your bonfire-coiffed attacker has only a superficial knowledge of it.

She's misquoting, so feel free to also correct her: "Pride goeth before a fall? Wrong, Jezebel! Pride goeth before destruction, and a haughty spirit before a fall." There were actually two Jezebels in the Bible, but as both were bad, feel free to use the name indiscriminately. At least in theory, your victim should know that she is being insulted either way. If you are concerned that she will miss your implication, replace "Jezebel" with "Whore of Babylon."

Cordially,

Lady Arabella Snark

Foe or Faux?

Test your knowledge of vituperation by determining if the following is an insult or not.

So I hear you were tripudiant last night, Juan. Is that true?

This is not an insult. Juan was dancing for joy.

Malediction 101: Holier than Thou

Just because your idea of "saved" means double coupon days at Sally's Ultra-Market, it doesn't mean you're a bad person. Likewise, while true believers deserve your respect, people who condemn you to a toasty afterlife while cutting in line for the portable bathroom at the revival meeting are asking for it. Have a little fun at their expense with these unusual words.

Oh, sister! You are as full of the Holy Spirit as the ancient *Chelonians!*

chelonian: the reptile family that includes turtles and tortoises

You're so right—those transgressors who put graven images like inflatable snowmen in their yards during the holidays are headed for the gates of hell. Only spotless souls like you deserve gifts of ancient *anthracite* for Christmas.

anthracite: hard coal

Oh, don't worry about stepping on my Bible, Doris. Those *ungulate* shoes really show your true religious character.

ungulate: hoof-shaped

Yes, I'm sure you didn't mean to brush up against my breast while you were passing the collection plate. You are a man like the *Acrasiomycetes* of old.

acrasiomycete: a kind of slime mold

If only I could blot out my sins with this handkerchief and be as pure as you, Aaron. I know that when you die, the place you go will be the opposite of *gelid!*

gelid: very cold

Dealings with Gentlemen, Scholars, and Toads

Dear Lady Snark,

I know how to hold my own with the guys, but sometimes, I have to go to my daughter's school and listen to her tight-ass egghead teacher tell me all kinds of crap about how she's never going to go to college unless she starts turning in homework or something. Man, I just want to squash him like a bug. If I insult a smart guy, do I have to say something smart?

Stan

Chicago, Illinois

My Dear,

I know exactly what you are talking about. At least twice a year, I am called upon to visit the dean of my stepson Eric's current university to discuss how his poor grades are increasing the likelihood that he will come home and live with me forever, like a sofa-bound, corn-chip-eating albatross. Naturally, I do not wish for this to happen while I am busy trying to find a new husband. There are few things as unattractive to potential mates as the fact that one is still caring for the offspring of one's deceased spouses because it reminds them that one's former spouses are deceased.

Foe or Faux?

Test your knowledge of vituperation by determining if the following is an insult or not.

I'm sorry, Gerard, but would you mind not bloviating at the dinner table?

This is an insult. To bloviate is to speak in a pompous manner.

Since this is quite similar to your situation, I will share a few pointers on how I deal with such persons. If it seems that there is still a chance bribery will work with said dean, I generally want to avoid any antagonism and instead couch my entreaties in the most complaisant terms. For example:

"My son is really quite bright, but he was distracted from studying by the fascinating social events, rich diversity of the student body, and beauty of the campus, which I would like to add to by donating enough money for a lovely new library."

However, if I sense my next move will be yet another pleading phone call to yet another small, private, overpriced New England liberal arts college that admits any student who has enough money and connections to spend the next six years studying Nihilism in the Films of Jackie Chan, I feel free to say whatever I wish.

As for you, if you are in a private meeting (as will most likely be your case) you may go for the element of surprise and use a vulgar profanity. This technique is entirely suitable for your purposes and you do not need to work any harder. In fact, trying to match wits with someone who might be above your mental station can backfire on you, as one brilliant memorized phrase will not stave off the endless highbrow comebacks your daughter's teacher may have up his double-knit polyester sleeve.

Public meetings are a different story. Using a coarse insult against the dean at a Parent's Weekend luncheon (or in your case, against the teacher at a PTA meeting) is not recommended as it has the downside of making you look, well, coarse. This matters when some of the other parents may be called upon to serve as character witnesses in your next murder trial.

Know Your Classical Languages

When you have an audience, I recommend the "shock and awe" technique. In this method, you throw out an extremely obscure slight, then toss your head disdainfully and haughtily flee the vicinity. By the time your opponent has figured out whether he should feel humiliated, you'll be halfway through the mini bar back at your hotel room. (Note: This tactic is far more successful in personal confrontations than international disputes.)

Greek and Latin words about animals are particularly fun to use for this type of assault, because no one remembers what the Romans called raccoons (except for classicists and zoologists, that is: Check on your victim's academic credentials before launching any of these attacks).

No doubt you are familiar with the basics: leonine (like a lion), bovine (like a cow), and hippopotamic (like a hippopotamus). But there are hundreds of such words for specific species! You don't even need to use one with an insulting meaning. Some of the worst-sounding adjectives are the most innocuous. For example:

> **What you say:** Why Molly, what a remarkably turdine dress that is!
>
> **What Molly hears:** Your dress looks like feces!

> **What it really means:** Molly, that dress reminds me of a wood thrush!
>
> **What you say:** Adam, you move in such an elaphine way.
>
> **What Adam hears:** You're as clumsy as an elephant.
>
> **What it really means:** Adam, you walk as gracefully as a stag through the forest.

But enough of faux cruelty! It's better to use the genuinely nasty terms on the following page if you really want to get your turdine victim's goat, so to speak.

I must tell my maid to get my things ready now as I am late for a little meeting with my parole officer, Delilah. But Stan, stick to this advice and try not to do anything asinine, however tempted you are! Assaulting public school teachers carries a heavy penalty as it is so difficult to find new ones to replace them—apparently it has something to do with the low pay, long hours, physical danger, and lack of respect.

Cordially,

Lady Arabella Snark

Quiz I Know You're Suidian, But What Am I?

See if you can match these insulting terms to their meanings.

1. ___ Darling, your skin looks positively eusuchian!   A.   like a snake

2. ___ When it comes to money, you are as hirudinal as they come!   B.   like a raccoon

3. ___ You remind me of my ex-husband. You're both so pediculine.   C.   like an alligator

4. ___ Oh, did you really enjoy that film? I found it a bit meleagrine.   D.   like a hog

5. ___ Your behavior toward me has been so elapoid this evening. Did you hear something about me and your husband?   E.   like a turkey

6. ___ I've never seen anyone quite so suidian at the buffet table!   F.   like a worm

7. ___ I try to give mature, caprine gentlemen like yourself all the room you need on the sofa.   G.   like a snail

8. ___ New makeup? You look so procyonid!   H.   like a goat

9. ___ Generally, I don't spend a great deal of time around vermian persons like yourself, but then I only seem to run into you when it rains.   I.   like a leech

10. ___ Still haven't finished that project from last year? How limacine you are.   J.   like a louse

Answer Key: 1. C; 2. I; 3. J; 4. E; 5. A; 6. D; 7. H; 8. B; 9. F; 10. G;

A Brief Note on Telephone Etiquette

Dear Lady Snark,

I like to think I am pretty patient, but sometimes, I just don't know how to respond to other people's rudeness. This morning, I was at a local café studying for a sociology exam when this woman started talking on her cell phone to her friend and boasting in a loud voice about how great her new job was and how much money she was going to make so everyone within earshot would be impressed. She just went on and on and on until all I could think about was punching her. At one point, I considered grabbing the cell phone and using it to beat her senseless, but I know this is probably not the most effective way to deal with the problem. What do you suggest?

Midori

Cambridge, Massachusetts

My Dear,

Your instincts are spot-on about the ineffectiveness of this course of action. Recent advances in technology have greatly reduced the size and heft of cellular telephones, rendering them utterly useless for making others aware of your displeasure. A heavy coffee mug, laptop computer, or chair would be far superior for this purpose.

Cordially,

Lady Arabella Snark

The Quixotic *Quiz*

Test Your Knowledge of Grammar, the Bible, Rocks, and Greek

1. Two of these three sentences are about grammar. Which one describes a sexual perversion?

    A. Lucie uses the genitive all the time, but then again, she's French.

    B. The way Gareth talked about copulas disgusted me.

    C. When Mason's statements became paraphilic, I left.

2. Identify which of the following words in the left-hand column describes a person from the Old Testament and which is the name of a rock.

	Old Testament	Rocks
Kenite	_____	_____
Amalekite	_____	_____
Malachite	_____	_____
Kyanite	_____	_____
Thulite	_____	_____
Amorite	_____	_____
Edomite	_____	_____
Zeolite	_____	_____

3. Choose the best word to complete the sentence.

I don't want him for my roommate because he's a(n)_____.

A. ichthyophile

B. scoptophile

C. typophile

D. logophile

Answer Key: 1. C. A paraphile enjoys deviant sexual practices. The genitive case indicates possession (e.g., "the agonies of my aunt") and a copula is used to connect the subject and complement of a sentence (e.g., "Jim is a loser"). 2. Kenites, Amalekites, Amorites, and Edomites were peoples in the Old Testament; malachite, thulite, kyanite, and zeolite are minerals. 3. Most likely B, depending on your predilections. A scoptophile is a voyeur. Ichthyophiles, typophiles, and logophiles love fish, typography, and words, respectively.

three. The High Price of Free Food

In which the philosophy of THOMAS HOBBES, the symbiotic relationships of MARINE LIFE, & the duties and responsibilities of BEING A GUEST are expounded upon, including rejecting invitations, understanding FRENCH, & avoiding situations likely to make you feel BLENNOPHOBIC.

The Cocktail Party: Nasty, Brutish, and Never Short Enough

When I think of entertaining, I think of cocktail parties; when I think of cocktail parties, I think of Thomas Hobbes, the seventeenth-century philosopher who believed that a person's life was, by nature "solitary, poor, nasty, brutish, and short" (which would also describe my fourth husband, Derrick).

According to Hobbes, this unfortunate state of affairs forces us to make a "social contract," happily tossing aside our personal freedoms in hopes that our lives will become communal, rich, pleasant, sophisticated, and long.

This social contract business is clearly a mistake. First of all, one of the rules we follow to attain a so-called pleasant life is to attend social gatherings (the horrors of which are only slightly dulled by copious amounts of alcohol) without following our natural impulse to kill the other guests indiscriminately.

And if one applies the quote to cocktail parties, since when is "solitary" a bad thing? Once you have spent an hour listening to someone recount how the size of each fish caught on their last holiday relates to the proportions of their children, pets, and body parts, standing in the corner by yourself with a martini begins to look quite attractive.

But we still go to them because otherwise, we would be forced to spend thousands of dollars a month on our own gin and troll the overpriced and tacky Riviera for suitable husbands. Reciprocally, wealthy people ask social scavengers to their parties to admire their new interior decoration and feed their egos, just as sharks allow those icky-looking little fish to clean their teeth unmolested. This is the great and interconnected "circle of life" you read about in sappy women's magazines when you are waiting interminably at the doctor's office and there is nothing else to do.

Of course, there are more disadvantages to attending parties than I have previously mentioned. In addition to the obligation of cleaning your host's teeth, you might also feel that you should bring a bottle of wine, buy them flowers, or send them a thank-you note.

All of these will strike you as repellent and you might be inclined to therefore avoid parties at all costs. However, there are more advantages than the free liquor. For one, as Hobbes so eloquently put it: "Laughter is nothing else but sudden glory arising from some sudden conception of some eminency in ourselves, by comparison with the infirmity of others." If you find Hobbes a bit highbrow, what he is trying to say is, "I laugh because other people have crappier lives than mine."

This, then, is the true beauty of the party: It gathers together an assortment of persons whom you may consider inferior. And what is a short, nasty, brutish life, after all, without opportunities to drunkenly ridicule our infirm, stupid, ugly, and otherwise repugnant peers?

Voulez-Vous Attendez Ma Soirée Dégueulasse?

Dear Lady Snark,

I went to a lot of parties in college, but people would just call me up or ask me in person. Sometimes, they'd send an e-mail to everybody. Now I'm working at my first job and I got a printed invitation to a party from my boss that says "RSVP." Is that some kind of password that people used to get into those rave parties they had in the old days?

Barry

Kaaawa, Hawaii

Foe or Faux?

Test your knowledge of vituperation by determining if the following is an insult or not.

Why, darling, how callipygian you look—just like the hos in that new rap video by Dawg-E Pound!

This is not an insult. To be callipygian is to have attractively shaped buttocks.

My Dear,

No, RSVP is not part of the strange secret language of brain-damaged former ecstasy addicts of a certain age (by which I mean older than you and younger than your parents).

Rather, RSVP is part of a strange secret language called "French." This obscure code, once essential to those working in international trade and pornography, used to be a marker of sophistication. Thus were mysterious phrases from it inserted into every British novel for six hundred years with the principal aim of making their authors feel smugly superior and readers who did not study it in finishing school feel insecure and moronic. Now, it is useful only for impressing dates with your knowledge of wine, cheese, or unusual sexual positions.

Roughly translated, RSVP means, "Tell me if you are coming or not, because as vile as it will be for you to have to eat reheated wholesale club 'pigs in blankets' made from unidentifiable chicken parts at the party, it would be far worse if I had so many left over that I was obliged to eat them myself."

By the way, if I have made you feel insecure and moronic because you cannot understand the title of this letter, it was purely intentional. It means "Would you like to come to my disgusting party?" Don't bother memorizing it to save yourself pain in the future; unfortunately, people are rarely so honest about what you should expect.

Cordially,

Lady Arabella Snark

Foe or Faux?

Test your knowledge of vituperation by determining if the following is an insult or not.

I never would have thought of serving cupcakes at a formal occasion. They're quite esculent.

This is not an insult. Esculent means edible.

When Hell Freezes Over: Declining Invitations

Dear Lady Snark,

I have a question about answering invitations. It's easy to say "no" if I have something else to do, but what can I do when I don't want to go to my coworker Mike's barbecue and I don't have a really good excuse? His parties are always awful and the last time he made hamburgers, they were raw in the middle. If I say "no" he'll want to know why and if I lie, he might find out I just stayed home and watched TV.

Chuck

Elk City, Oklahoma

My Dear,

May I assume that you are afraid of hurting his feelings? How quaint! I should point out to you that making Mike feel wretched will forestall any future unwanted invites, but I understand. You wish to be "polite." This is a complex issue, so let us begin by examining how the type of invitation influences the ease of rejection.

The Oral Invitation:

If you are asked to an event in person, you should simply demur, explaining that such decisions must be made by someone with more authority, such as your girlfriend or parole officer. If pressed later, you can say that you have been denied permission and sadly, it is out of your hands.

The Online Invitation:

For younger persons who use the Internet, technology provides an easy out. Most online invitations offer a full view of the guest list, information on who has and has not accepted the invitation, and the option of replying "maybe" rather than "yes" or "no." Choose "maybe" when what you really mean is, "I suppose I could grace you with my presence if one of the other three people of worth on this list announces they are going to be there. Otherwise, I will stay at home and clean the toilet."

The Posted Invitation:

If the invitation comes in the mail, you are expected to respond in kind. Written invitations therefore introduce a new problem: It is important to know the right kind of paper on which to write refusals. If you do not wish to offend, use nice, heavy cream-colored stationery and write your answer with a quill or fountain pen. For those whose feelings you don't mind squashing, the back of a dry cleaning receipt will suffice. No need for an envelope—just stuff it into their pocket when they aren't looking.

And now to the actual wording of your answer. If you accept, little is asked of you. You may simply say: "I am looking forward to the tedious conversation and stale hors d'oeuvres I've come to expect from you and Paul. See you Saturday!"

Foe or Faux?

Test your knowledge of vituperation by determining if the following is an insult or not.

Your cocktail parties are marvelous. I always feel so crapulent afterwards!

This is not an insult. To become crapulent, simply overindulge in food and drink. That your host has provided this opportunity is a good thing.

Yes, I Like Cannolis, But That's an Offer I Can Refuse

Saying "no" requires more effort, and this is something hosts are foolishly counting on: that some will come to the party rather than agonize over a polite rejection. In reality, most of these people will simply "forget" the invitation in a trash bin or pretend they never received it.

I am sure you are above such childishness. Besides, letting the host know why you will not come might help him or her to improve their hosting skills for the next event. The general structure of the polite refusal is as follows. First, thank the host for the invitation.

> **Dear Janie, Thank you so much for inviting me to your daughter's "coming out" party. I am glad that you have finally come to terms with her sexual orientation.**

....

(Of course, Janie means no such thing by "coming out party." She wants me to witness the train wreck of her potato-faced teenage daughter's introduction to society with some sort of insipid dance that will introduce her to rich, eligible, pimply boys.)

Second, state directly that you will not be attending. You should indicate that you regret this, whether or not it is true.

> **I am terribly sorry that I will not be there for this monumental rite of passage . . .**

....

Third, it is generally expected that you will provide an explanation for why you cannot be there. Normally, polite would-be guests use the excuse that they have prior plans.

➤ . . . because I have an appointment for a colonoscopy, which I have been looking forward to for some time.

Note that the nature of your prior plans may influence the likelihood of your receiving another invitation and plan accordingly. If you feel it would be helpful, you may note additional reasons for your disinclination to spend time in their company.

➤ Besides, I don't think your husband has gotten over my recent abandonment of his attentions in favor of my tennis instructor and I do not wish to endure his hangdog looks all evening.

Examples of Appropriate Rejections with "Really Good Excuses"
It is, indeed, an onerous task to reject people, and you have my permission to use the same generic excuse (such as having a manicure at Brenda's House of Beauty) for every occasion (such as a tailgate party or funeral). Another option is to use your knowledge of Greek word roots to fashion a conveniently obscure and unverifiable

phobia that prevents you from gracing the event with your presence. Should you decide to go this route, I have included a little phobia quiz to amuse you on page 65. However, if you genuinely wish to be thoughtful, Chuck, you will take care to craft event-appropriate excuses, as shown below.

The Cocktail Party:
How devastated I am to say that I will not be present at your petite soirée on June 10th. Unfortunately, the exceptionally weak drinks you ordinarily serve at these occasions are not sufficient to dull my senses to your boyfriend's futile efforts to grope me in the hallway.

The House Party:
As distasteful as it is to decline your invitation, I'm afraid that it is preferable to attending yet another half-assed weekend eating gunky canapés in that cesspool of a shack you call a beach cottage.

The Keg Party:
Words cannot express my disappointment that I must pass on the invitation to once again witness your gelatinous buttocks

swaying as you try to climb a greased pole naked in search of athletic glory. Sadly, the last occasion on which I witnessed this event had a deleterious effect on my psyche for which I am still seeking the attention of a therapist.

The Quinceañera:
While I regret the opportunity to have a limb sheared off by the ginormous starched ruffles on your daughter Anna's poufy dance dress, I'm afraid I would rather be a piñata in the land of the giants.

The Children's Birthday Party:
Oh, the agony of being denied the pleasure of your company on Sunday for Jimmy's first birthday! If only I had already lost the upper register of my hearing, I too could enjoy the spectacle of him playing for hours with an empty cardboard box instead of the costly gift it once contained.

The Fraternity Hazing:
How kind of you to invite me to join your fraternity. I was truly afraid that my three-digit IQ might disqualify me from membership, so I really appreciate your overlooking it! As much as I am grateful for the chance to decrease that number

by drinking a bottle of Scotch by myself, I will have to decline as I get terribly carsick, especially when lying prone in the trunk.

Foe or Faux?

Test your knowledge of vituperation by determining if the following is an insult or not.

I'm so sorry I must leave. Your wife's conversation is positively logorrheic!

This is an insult. His wife's endless, incoherent rambling is the cause of your departure.

The Bachelor Party:
How modern of you to have a joint prenuptial bash with Karen that does not involve strippers, porno movies, or lavish amounts of alcohol! Unfortunately, I cannot be there as I am previously engaged for drinks and a lap dance with Dominique at the Silver Banana.

The Twenty-Fifth Wedding Anniversary:
It's wonderful that you and Lila have managed to stay together despite the affairs, the drug addiction, and the prison

sentence. Alas! Having been apprised of the menu, I will have to stay away as I am allergic to all foods containing mini marshmallows. However, I wish you twenty-five more years of equal "happiness."

The College Graduation:
I would love to be there for your son's important ceremony, but I'm afraid my unrestrained laughter at the notion of Biff getting a job would distract from the proceedings.

As for your specific situation, you may have by now formed an idea of how to respond. If not, I would suggest:

As much as I would enjoy consuming a pig that has been drawn, quartered, and scorched, I suspect that I would feel as though I'd undergone the same procedure after an hour or two at your party. Do enjoy yourself, and I will see you at work on Monday, if you are not in the hospital with E. coli.

Cordially,

Lady Arabella Snark

 **The Greek Way: Just Say No!**

Coming up with new and creative ways to evade objectionable social engagements can be such a chore, but here are ten excuses that your host probably hasn't heard before. See how many of these arcane phobias you can match to their meanings!

1.____ Darling, you know I'd love to come for the whole weekend, but I'm afraid my blennophobia would make it impossible for me to bathe in your tub.

2.____ I know that Marta has been your family's cook for years, but after witnessing her unusual bathroom rituals last month, I think I'll have to pass on dinner. You know how I suffer from mysophobia.

3.____ I wish I could make it to your "backyard cleanup" party, but I have ergophobia issues.

4.____ Grandmother Petra, it is always nice to see you, but your favorite eighties sweater, as well as it has held up, gives me optophobia, so I'll have to miss Thanksgiving.

A. fear of opening one's eyes

B. fear of sitting

C. fear of slime

D. fear of the moon

continued

5.___ Is your Uncle Grant, the personal injury lawyer, going to be at the party, too? You know, I think I should pass as I'm still undergoing treatment for selachophobia.

E.   fear of work

6.___ As delightful as your streaking party sounds, I must decline because of my selenophobia.

F.   fear of puppets

7.___ Oh, sorry, I can't. It's not my cathisophobia per se that keeps me standing up when I'm at your parties. It's the fact that your irritating sister Jemima is always on the sofa by the only empty space.

G.   fear of sharks

8.___ I love children's parties, but having heard about your entertainment plans, I cannot attend. My pupaphobia had been quite troublesome this month.

H.   fear of germs

Answer Key: 1. C; 2. H; 3. E; 4. A; 5. G; 6. D; 7. B; 8. F

The Dreaded High School Reunion

Dear Lady Snark,

I'm going to my fifth high school reunion next month! I'm really excited about it because I've lost a lot of weight and I have a girlfriend now, plus I'm in law school. I just don't want to rub it in too much and make the people who used to beat me up feel bad about being losers in comparison.

Just kidding! How long do you think I should wait before I start telling them about my being on the dean's list and all that stuff?

Gordon

Phoenix, Arizona

My Dear,

Do you remember when you were fifteen and the other boys gave you wedgies, pushed your head into the toilet, and wrote anonymous graffiti in the girls' locker room about your supposed genital deformities?

Trust me, so do they. I would try to dissuade you from your intended path by explaining that the more successful you've become, the more the toothless trailer-park bullies will want to shove your head in the toilet again. But I know I can't. I can only hope that something untoward, like a tsunami or tax audit, will prevent you from attending until the fifteenth or twentieth reunion, when they will be too old and fat to overpower you.

If you are determined, I can at least give you some advice regarding the other type of bully you are doomed to encounter. Oh, it's true that the genuinely successful members of your graduating class will be too busy to attend. But there will still be plenty of former cheerleaders and basketball stars there, flashing their glittering teeth as they tell stories that easily eclipse your modest accomplishments. These will seem so practiced that you might even think that their sole purpose in life for the last five years has been to prepare for this event, blowing themselves up like pufferfish to make you feel miserable.

You would be right—they have. But don't despair. While sushi chefs must pass rigorous certification classes to puncture and serve such animals, you can learn how to do it by following the example of Nate, whose story I will now recount.

Foe or Faux?

Test your knowledge of vituperation by determining if the following is an insult or not.

So, Raquel, I understand you and Tony spent your honeymoon on the Great Barrier Reef as urinators.

This is not an insult. Urinator is an antiquated term for diver.

Nate, like you, was of modest popularity in high school. He was treasurer of the AV club, wrote video game reviews for the school newspaper, and went to the prom with his reasonably attractive cousin Janet, who promptly deserted him to spend the evening dancing with Earl, the football star.

Nate's life has turned out well. He is now the owner of a successful computer repair shop, which he runs with his live-in girlfriend Marge. He stays fit and enjoys many social activities, such as Morris dancing, orienteering, and madrigal sing-a-longs. However, he sometimes wonders how his life compares to his former classmates and so decides to go to his tenth year reunion in Green Bay and find out.

He is about to learn the hard way that nothing has changed since high school. Just as it was when he was fifteen, the best defense is still to wield the sushi knife of crushing indifference. Attacks will only serve to demonstrate his jealousy and insecurity, and feed his rivals' feelings of superiority.

The Education of Stupid Nate

By sheer coincidence, Earl the football star is the first person Nate and Marge see when they arrive. He stands alone by the snack table (his wife Patty having left him the previous year for Stephanie, the prom queen) stuffing his rotund face with cheese curls and checking his PDA for nonexistent e-mail messages. Nate begins the conversation by asking Earl what he has been up to since they last saw one another at graduation.

66 **Earl: What have I done recently? Well, I've been pretty busy! I was made CEO of my company last year and I've been working eighty hours a week—though of course my seven-figure salary more than makes up for that. What have you been up to?**

Nate's natural (and stupid) reaction to this boast is to lie, while reaching casually for his own snack:

> **Stupid Nate: Not much. I won the Nobel Prize for chemistry last year, but now I'm trying to focus on bringing about world peace.**

At this point, Marge cringes with embarrassment, knowing that Earl can refute this information through his wireless connection before Nate has consumed a single chip. A better response would be this:

> **Smart Nate: That's so fantastic for you! I couldn't take a job like that—it's too important to me to have time to have a social life and, well, go to the gym. But congratulations! So where's Patty?**

Note that this works for Nate because of the enviable life he leads in comparison to Earl. If you are still single and spending most of your evenings in your parents' basement enchanting trolls in online fantasy games, you might want to make a more generalized comment about your reticence to give up the ability to take frequent and enjoyable vacations. You do not need to explain that they take place exclusively at science fiction conventions. Make your observation and quickly excuse yourself to discuss the technical merits of the sound system with the DJ.

Next, Nate meets Connor, who handily beat him out for a spot on the tennis team in his sophomore year.

> **Connor: Orienteering, huh? While summering in Africa last year, I summited Kilimanjaro!**
>
> **Stupid Nate: Big deal!**

....

Again, Nate has fallen prey to his own insecurity. This answer will make Connor smirk with delight as he flexes his bicep. Rather, Nate should appear to be pleased for Connor.

> **Smart Nate: Oh, I just saw a documentary on a man who did that without any arms or legs. It's wonderful that you could do it too!**

....

Russell, a former drum major, once punished Nate for goofing off during band practice by forcing him to run naked around the football field with his tuba, playing "Stars and Stripes Forever" until he passed out. Here he is now walking by Nate's table on his way to the exit.

> **Russell: Is this your wife? I married Peligriano, the Serbian supermodel.**
>
> **Stupid Nate: I like a woman with a little more meat on her bones, like Marge here.**

I do not need to explain Nate's mistake to you, I am sure. By avoiding this comment, he will retain enough teeth to smile conspiratorially and congratulate Russell on his good fortune.

> **Smart Nate: How nice! It's always easier to convince them you've got it when they don't speak English, eh?**

Finally, here is Joe, smirking by the punchbowl. In high school, Joe exploited his position as editor of the school yearbook to immortalize his enemies with unflattering photos, Nate's involving women's underwear worn involuntarily as a hat.

> **Joe:** My wife's Chinese Shar-Pei won best in show at the 87th Annual Trans-American Dog Show—but I'm sure you saw that on television.

Unfortunately, Nate is nervously thinking of his own mongrel, Fluffy, whose fur has mysteriously come off in patches this year.

> **Stupid Nate:** That competition has really gone to the dogs!

He should instead bestow this ambiguous compliment:

> **Smart Nate:** And what a bitch she is!

I hope that is helpful to you, dear, and that you will enjoy your reunion, though I think that's unlikely; developing a thick skin takes years of practice. So as a final piece of advice, I recommend that you first remove all sharp objects from your hotel room, so that you will be unable to hurt yourself after the party.

Cordially,

Lady Arabella Snark

Foe or Faux?

Test your knowledge of vituperation by determining if the following is an insult or not.

Mary, how charming of you to have made yourself more pulchritudinous for our bridge game.

This is not an insult. Mary has beautified herself.

Malediction 101: The Artfully Insulting Thank-You Letter

If you had a miserable evening out, but for some reason would like to keep a good relationship with your inept host, use the cryptic words in these insincere expressions of gratitude.

What a lovely evening last Friday was. Your entertainment left me with so many opportunities for *omphaloskepsis*!
omphaloskepsis: gazing at your navel

How splendid that your daughter could play the piano for us. Her recital was utterly *cacophonous*.
cacophonous: unpleasant and harsh sounding

It was so kind of you to show me your childhood scrapbook
all evening. I don't think I have ever felt so *somnolent*.
somnolent: drowsy

What an interesting brunch that was. I find your wife a
perfect *lamia*.
lamia: a vampire-like female monster

I was a bit surprised by some of the unique party games
you were so eager for us to try, but then again, you and
your wife are such *peccable* hosts!
peccable: inclined to sin

An Inquiry That Addresses the Mental Health Benefits of Red Wine

Dear Lady Snark,

I was at a party last weekend when suddenly, my companion nudged
me to draw my attention to Jodi McCall, who was just walking in. She

was wearing a beautiful pale-pink silk sheath by Marcus Michaels—the exact same dress I had on. Jodi walked in my direction to make sure I (and everyone else) had a good view and smirked as she passed me. All the other guests tittered behind their hands. I am sure she felt that the dress showed her "assets" to better advantage than it did mine, but I just drank my merlot and said nothing. I was mortified. My companion told me later that I should have said something to break the tension—a joke or witty little remark. What would have been the best thing to say?

Celia

Grosse Point, Michigan

My Dear,

The appropriate comment would have been, "Oops!" as you "accidentally" sloshed your merlot on her "assets." Like the Highlander, there can only be one. Next time, make sure it's you.

Cordially,

Lady Arabella Snark

The Quixotic *Quiz*

Test Your Knowledge of Popular French Phrases

. . . .

Should you wish to move in the first circles of société, it will be necessary for you to know more Français than RSVP. Test your readiness by seeing how many of these French phrases you can translate correctly.

1. If you are at a dinner party and someone says, "Passez-moi le sel, s'il vous plaît" they are asking you to

    A. braid their hair.

    B. pass the salt.

    C. engage in a sexual act under the table that is illegal in Texas, Alabama, and some parts of Kansas.

2. The feudal custom called "le droit du seigneur" is

    A. still practiced in Provence.

    B. now a popular party game.

    C. unfortunate if you are not the seigneur.

3. Crudités are

   A. raw vegetables.

   B. pornographic postcards.

   C. what your husband utters when he has had too much to drink.

4. "Après moi, le déluge" is

   A. a typical toast in France.

   B. a phrase that means, "Please go ahead of me."

   C. something you should not say to other guests when you are leaving the bathroom.

5. You are at a party when the host's sophisticated friend points at a chair and says, "I believe that piece is fin de siècle. What do you think?" The correct answer is

   A. "Um, it's pretty."

   B. "Oh, totally. It looks just like a shark."

   C. "Espèce de crétin! It's clearly early Victorian."

Answer key: 1. B; 2. C. "Droit de seigneur" refers to the right of the feudal lord to sleep with a bride before her unfortunate serf husband. 3. A; 4. C. "Après moi, le déluge" were the prophetic words of Louis XV, referring to the coming revolution in eighteenth-century France. While the phrase literally means, "After me, the flood," indoor plumbing was unknown at Versailles. 5. C. "Fin de siècle" means end of the nineteenth century. "Espèce de crétin" is a fancy way of saying idiot.

four. The Hostess with the Mostess Is the Vamp Who Has Decamped

In which Lady Snark entertains the reader with horrific cautionary tales of BEING A HOST, involving PICKLED GUESTS, KABUKI THEATER, & DULL CLICHÉS; in addition, the reader's ability to solve LOGIC PROBLEMS about SEASONAL VEGETABLES is tested.

Why Not to Invite People to Your Home, Ever

Since this is a book of manners, many people will assume that I plan to encourage my readers to entertain. Nothing could be further from the truth; hosting parties can lead to financial ruin, social disgrace, and worse, an empty liquor cabinet. This is a lesson I learned in my extreme youth, when I was stupid and occasionally felt compelled to share my inebriants with others.

Shortly after I married my first husband, Arthur, he decided that we should live in Cowslip, a dully quaint Connecticut town possessed of a second-rate university, where he was on the faculty in the linguistics department. With nothing else to do in this dreary New England hamlet but shop from catalogs, redecorate, and drink, I spent the next year of my life seeking entertainment from the paltry university library and various attractive young doctoral candidates in Arthur's department.

Once I had run out of students and read all of the library's books once and some twice (including three fascinating tomes on gerund formation in Madagascar) I became bored and decided I would ask some of Arthur's colleagues over to the house for a convivial evening. I had thought it would be fun because I'd seen photos of elegant hostesses in the society pages, and it didn't seem like much work. In anticipation of an intellectual salon, I spent all day overseeing Arthur as he prepared the hors d'oeuvres.

Foe or Faux?

Test your knowledge of vituperation by determining if the following is an insult or not.

I'm not sure you should come over for dinner. Cedric told me you were an oenophile.

This is not an insult. An oenophile is a wine lover; the speaker doubts her beverage selection would be sufficiently sophisticated for such a guest.

It took me only a few hours to learn that guests do not come to your home because they like you. They come because they are hoping that if they drain enough tiki glasses filled with Mai Tais, going home with their own spouse will seem marginally less objectionable than driving their car into a tree. Due to the alcoholic content of Mai Tais, these two events sometimes overlap.

To be honest, you are lucky if they leave. Most of them will still be there at three in the morning, propositioning your husband, blathering on about their work with chromosomes, and throwing up before they fall asleep on your bathroom floor.

My first party was essentially the end of my entertaining career and I think you would be very wise to end yours now, before you start. However, if you are still hell-bent on trying out one of these little fêtes for yourself, I have included some helpful hints in this chapter. You might also wish to purchase good homeowner's insurance—the kind that would cover, say, the accidental death of a guest.

As for those hostesses in the society pages, remember that they do not cook, clean, or serve. If they are smiling in the photos, it is because they are hopped up to the gills on prescription medications.

I'd Rather Have a Bottle in Front of Me

Dear Lady Snark,

I'm having a cocktail party for about two dozen people this Thursday. I'm going to serve some hors d'oeuvres and I think I have that part figured out, but I'm not sure how much liquor to buy. Can you give me an estimate?

Katie

Ann Arbor, Michigan

My Dear,

How unfortunate that you have gotten yourself into this nightmare situation. The idea is to attend cocktail parties, not to host them. That's money you could be spending on having your face redone, though given your address, perhaps you are one of those bookish types who just doesn't care.

Since you are committed to this folly, I will provide you with a simple formula. For each person, you should figure four normal mixed drinks (six ounces of alcohol). Add ten ounces for each guest who has recently completed a drug or alcohol rehabilitation program; twelve for each guest who finds their cat more entrancing than George Clooney; and sixteen for each guest whose ex-boyfriend, also in attendance, now dresses as a woman. Add these figures up to find the total amount of liquor you will personally want to consume during the evening. Multiply that figure by three and you will have the necessary amount for everyone. Be sure to drink most of your portion before the other guests arrive to ensure a carefree evening.

Cordially,

Lady Arabella Snark

Accidents Happen if You Work Hard Enough to Make Them

Dear Lady Snark,

Two months ago, my partner Ruben and I moved to an upscale condo downtown. It's on the ninth floor and has a spectacular view of the water. Our problem is our new neighbor, Althea. Whenever we have a party, she gets incredibly drunk and acts like an idiot, but since she lives next door, it's really hard to keep her from coming. Last week, she finished off a bottle of gin by herself before bursting into tears, flinging the French doors open to the night, and telling anyone who would listen that she was going to give birth to Jesus later that evening.

Ruben thinks we should just tell her to go to hell, but I was brought up to be a gentleman. Even when she does something really awful, like coming on to me, I want to say something more polite, like "Althea, while I appreciate the offer to 'sample your wares,' you are simply too anesthetized to know what you are doing. Please desist!" What do you think?

Tom

Seattle, Washington

Foe or Faux?

Test your knowledge of vituperation by determining if the following is an insult or not.

Look at your husband enjoying snacks with his friends. How frugivorous he is!

This is not an insult. Her husband is eating fruit.

My Dear,

I think your best bet would be to invite her again, leave the French doors open and remark casually that you doubt she could fly out over the Space Needle. (Not loudly enough that anyone could hear you, of course.)

But I jest! You are obviously too "nice" to rid yourself of this gin-guzzling albatross in that manner. In fact, you are probably thinking right now about the odds that an innocent bystander might be crushed, rather than the more important concern that such a person could break her fall.

You really need to practice being more forthright. A better version of your admonition would be:

No one is interested in licking you, Althea, despite the fact that you are more sauced than a Christmas goose!

The problem with using the elegant terms you seem to favor is that drunks have a hard time understanding the basics. There's no reason to beat around the bush.

Wrong: Your dipsomaniacal tendencies are wreaking havoc with our soirées, Althea.

Right: You're a lush!

Wrong: Perhaps you have already imbibed enough, my dear.

Right: If you were any more marinated, we could grill you on the barbecue.

Wrong: Your intoxicated cavorting is reminiscent of a barnyard animal.

Right: You're more shitfaced than a three-legged pig.

Wrong: I can only hope that the prodigious quantity of spirits you've quaffed will serve to embalm you.

Right: Die, you old hooch hound!

Foe or Faux?

Test your knowledge of vituperation by determining if the following is an insult or not.

Janice, I'd love for you to come to my husband's seventy-fifth birthday party, but as you are suffering from agerasia, I think you should probably stay away.

This is not an insult. The speaker is concerned about having Janice near her husband because she looks very young for her age.

I'm going to stop now because I'm being called away by an extra-dry martini, but I do hope that you will keep working at this until you can actually hurt someone intentionally without apologizing. By the way, should you ever get to the level at which you are ready to take my initial advice, please let me know so that I can avoid your street on the evening in question.

Cordially,

Lady Arabella Snark

Malediction 101: Painted Ladies

Hosting parties is painful. Brighten your evening with these observations on the unfortunate physical appearances of your female guests!

No, there's nothing in my eye. I'm experiencing involuntary spasms as the *coruscation* of your green eye shadow scorches my retinas.
coruscation: glittering or flashing

If you have some spackle in your purse, you might want to touch up your foundation. A *crevasse* is beginning to form on your forehead.
crevasse: a mountaineering term for a deep crack or chasm

How can you say Victoria's makeup is garish?! I am sure she is scheduled for a *Kabuki* performance later in the evening.
Kabuki: a form of Japanese theater in which actors wear stylized, mask-like makeup.

Oh, you're looking for Mitzi? I'm afraid your unsubtle cosmetics have triggered her acute *coulrophobia*. I'm sure she'll come out from under the sofa when you've moved on to the library.
coulrophobia: an irrational fear of clowns

Darling, would you mind turning a little more toward me? I'm recharging my mobile phone's *photovoltaic* battery with the glaring reflection of the candelabra on your oily nose.
photovoltaic: producing voltage when exposed to a light source

Party Like There's No Tomorrow until the Cows Come Home? Like Hell!

Dear Lady Snark,

My wife and I are hosting a party on the patio this coming Saturday. The problem is that I'm a little embarrassed by the way she tries to make small talk. Everything she says is a cliché. The whole evening is going to be: "Another guest? Any friend of yours is a friend of mine"; "Sure, use the phone. No skin off my nose!"; and "Man, I'm just running around with this iced tea like a chicken with its head cut off!" Her absolute favorite is "like hell!" which she adds to every other sentence. Could you give me some ideas on how to improve the situation?

Max

Pawtucket, Rhode Island

My Dear,

You can't pull the wool over my eyes! You're hoping I'll recommend a divorce. Like hell! But don't worry—we'll correct that problem in two shakes of a lamb's tail.

"Like hell" is quite useful, but hell no longer emits the pungent, acrid, and threatening smell it did back in the Middle Ages, when people suffered regular hallucinations brought on by improperly stored grains. I suppose you could heighten the impact of your wife's "like hell" clichés by feeding your guests deli sandwiches made with ergot-infected rye bread. However, it takes less effort to simply replace "like hell" with something that paints a more vivid picture. Here are some examples:

Wrong: You look like hell.

Right: You look like Marie Schaeffer-Stein after a handful of downers and a pool party.

Wrong: Your Scotch tastes like hell.

Right: Your Scotch tastes like the inside of the toilets in the bathroom at CBGB, which I was forced to lick in 1992 as part of my fraternity hazing for Phi Kappa Pu.

Wrong: You think you have a chance at becoming chair of the Springfield Historical Society? Like hell!

Right: You have as much chance of becoming chair of the Springfield Historical Society as you have of fitting into a size two dress without cutting off one of your legs.

Wrong: Sitting through Simone's third wedding was like hell.

Right: Sitting through Simone's third wedding was almost as much fun as getting poked in the eye with a shard of wicker basket by Betsy, the hyperactive flower girl, at her second.

If your wife can't bring herself to be creative, don't throw out the baby with the bathwater. Clichés are not always bad and even a broken watch is correct twice a day.

Cordially,

Lady Arabella Snark

....

1. Mary needs seven cans of green beans. If Mary can only carry two cans at a time, how many round trips does she need to make to the supermarket?

   A. Three trips

   B. Four trips

   C. Five trips

   D. Doesn't Mary have a car?

   E. Why on earth is Mary eating green beans from a can?

   F. Please tell me she isn't buying such large quantities because she is planning to serve them to guests!

2. Alex likes champagne but not potato chips. He likes caviar but not pigs in blankets. He likes candied violets but not pretzels. Alex probably wouldn't like

   A. crème caramel

   B. truffles

   C. my party

3. You are having a party on Friday. You normally drink four Scotches (three ounces each) per party, which is one-fifth of what Gary drinks, but Harlan drinks seven times as much as you. If Ken drinks ten times as much Gary, and Mike drinks four times as much as Ken and Harlan combined, how much Scotch do you need to buy for Mike?

   A.   a fifth

   B.   two gallons

   C.   I think it goes without saying that I didn't invite that bunch of alkies to my party.

4. It is the end of the evening and your husband's mistress is walking out of the front door with her car keys, utterly incapacitated with drink and compelled, because of a construction project detour, to drive home on a poorly lighted, narrow, winding mountain road that has no guard rails. What is your legal responsibility?

   A.   I need to keep her from leaving because I am liable if she is stopped by the police.

   B.   I need to keep her from leaving because I am liable if she drives off a cliff.

   C.   Oh, did she leave already? I must have been in the kitchen.

Answer Key: 1. F,; 2. C; 3. C; 4. C

five. Love Is Never Having to Say I'm Sorry
for Cheating on You with Your Brother

In which the reader is edified in all matters relating to COURTSHIP
& MARRIAGE, including RABIES, TERRORISTS, ANALOGIES, BACKHANDED
COMPLIMENTS, & ancient REDWOOD TREES.

The Unfortunate Effects of Hydrophobia on May-December Relationships

In Zora Neale Hurston's Harlem Renaissance masterpiece, *Their Eyes Were Watching God*, middle-aged heroine Janie snares Tea Cake, a good-looking man half her age with nothing better to do than spend hours combing out her hair. I did not read this book myself, but my stepdaughter Amelia did in prep school and she felt compelled to quote passages so extensively at the breakfast table during her spring break that I felt I had.

Unlike my naïve stepdaughter, I accurately predicted that Tea Cake would be trouble later on. Entanglements with younger men are always problematic when based on love; if they are only there for the money, it is easier to send them away when they become tiresome or start frothing at the mouth and trying to kill you, as Janie's boy toy eventually does.

Alas, Janie does not sense trouble. Since her previous husband often "played the dozens" at her expense, she has fairly low expectations. Often played on street corners and in junior high school cafeterias, playing the dozens is a verbal competition in which opponents match wits in an effort to rip one another to emotional shreds. In this way, it shares many elements with word games in my own social circle, such as "Dictionary," "Anagrams," and "What does this clause in the prenup really mean?"

Foe or Faux?

Test your knowledge of vituperation by determining if the following is an insult or not.

Whenever I look at your ruby lips, I think of a carbuncle!

This could be an insult. A carbuncle can be a lovely red garnet, but it can also be a large, swollen, oozing infection. You might, therefore, want clarification on this comment.

Since Teacake refrains from employing "snaps" against his beloved, he seems like a winner. He does not say, for example, that Janie is so unattractive that she must wear a necklace of filet mignon to attract the family dog's attention. Nor does he mention that that her mother is so obese she must accessorize her ensemble with an asteroid belt, or that her father suffers from such substandard intelligence that he is regularly injured by stationary automobiles. However, his aforementioned rabidity becomes problematic and she is finally obliged to shoot her little bonbon in self defense, ending up in jail.

This isn't to say that one should avoid May-December relationships; it is just that you should never enter into a romantic partnership without adequate legal representation. If only Janie had scouted out a good attorney before becoming attached to a juvenile Lothario, she would have been swiftly exonerated and back on the social circuit within a few hours of the incident, as I was in Paris in 1983 after the "accidental" shooting death of my attractive, blackmailing aerobics instructor.

In affairs of the heart, youth and beauty are ephemeral, charm often false, and promises of undying love easily overridden by the sudden appearance of someone half your age with twice your cleavage. However, if you keep a cool head and base your romantic attachments on age, infirmity, and real estate holdings, you will never be disappointed.

The Heaving Alabaster Bosoms of Amarillo, Texas

Dear Lady Snark,

My wife, Mabel, writes books—they're all the same story about an English girl who marries some rich guy who rides a big horse and has castles all over the place even though he gambles pretty much every day. Before they get married, the girl and "milord" spend 400 pages drinking rum punch and talking to each other with their eyebrows arched "ironically."

Anyway, here's the problem: She's supposed to be the keynote speaker at a romance writers' conference in Texas next weekend and she wants me to go with her. First of all, I kind of had a thing with her friend Sandy last year and I'm pretty sure she's going to be there so it could get ugly. Plus, when Mabel and her writer friends get together, they talk like those dumb British movies where all the women sit around complaining because they only have six maids, so I'm not going to understand a word anybody says to me. I'm just an insurance salesman, you know? I don't think I can get out of going, but maybe you can clue me in to the lingo. I'd appreciate it.

Todd

Hannibal, Missouri

My Dear,

You are in trouble. This is pretty much how I see your weekend turning out:

In the sultry air of Amarillo, Sandy Keebler (a.k.a. Morgana Hyatt-Pryce) fans herself with a dainty hand as she reclines on a faux-brocade beach towel, her creamy white skin tempting the gods. Incredulous to discover this wanton vixen in a leopard-print bathing suit that borders on licentiousness, Todd readily agrees to her offer of a glass of port.

Soon heady with wine, he gallantly embarks on a poolside flirtation, only to be observed in this compromising tête-à-tête by his wife, Mabel Greenblatt (a.k.a. Elizabeth Vere de Vere) who cannot help but feel an agonizing pain twisting her heart until it is ready to cleave in two. Todd was the only man she had ever loved, the only man who could control the wild passions of her heart.

And so on. I really think you should stay home. But if you, unlike Lord Penderly (the hero of Morgana's bestseller *Marry a Rakehell*), cannot best your wife in an argument, I will try to help by supplying you with translations of some of the language you are likely to hear in the heated exchange that will no doubt follow. At least then you will understand why you are being divorced.

Mabel: Doxy! You may believe you have stolen my husband, but you are nothing more than a dressy bit of muslin to him.

Translation: Slut! My husband won't leave me. He just wants to screw you.

Sandy: I've no objection to a libertine. At least then I would not be bored.

Translation: Like I care about that.

Mabel: You are insufferable, rattlepated strumpet!

Translation: I hate you, stupid whore.

Sandy: Leave us, vexatious harridan. I am beginning to feel indisposed.

Translation: Get lost, irritating old bitch. You're making me sick.

Mabel: You care for nothing but what you can find in a pair of inexpressibles!

Translation: You just want to get into some guy's pants.

Sandy: I cannot refute it.
Translation: You got that right, sister!

Mabel: Todd, do not forget who holds the purse strings! If you do not come hither this instant, upon my honor, I will deal you a blow with my reticule that would impress Mr. Jackson himself.
Translation: I'm the breadwinner in this family, Todd. Get your ass over here or I'll beat you senseless with my purse.

At this stage in the conversation, you would be wise to renounce any tender feelings you ever had for Sandy and her fetching leopard-print bathing suit and assure your wife that your impertinence will never again be repeated.

Then you might want to hit the bar for a large tumbler of Blue Ruin (a.k.a. gin) or, better yet, drink it in the privacy of your hotel room, as a conference of that nature is no doubt teeming with heaving bosoms, hot tempers, and excellent imaginations. Though you may not be a Corinthian of the first stare, the absence of testosterone at such an event might transform even a balding insurance agent of middle years into a swoon-inducing hero of yesteryear. Play it safe.

Cordially,

Lady Arabella Snark

Foe or Faux?

Test your knowledge of vituperation by determining if the following is an insult or not.

Rita, I think you should try to limit your heliolatry. It's making your skin coriaceous.

This is an insult. Rita's skin is leathery because she spends too much time worshiping the sun.

Malediction 101: Oh, How We Danced!

Dancing should be romantic, but if you find yourself staring in awestruck horror at your date's moves instead, feel free to use one of these lines to help them become aware of their choreographic deficiencies.

Stop touching yourself like that, Terry! This is not an *onanism* club.

onanism: the kind of self love that Father Timothy says can make you blind

Quiet, everyone! Based on those last moves, I think she's getting ready for the *glossolalia!*

glossolalia: speaking in tongues

I think I need to lie down. The *Brownian motion* of your belly fat is making me nauseous.

Brownian motion: a rapid, random, and vibrating movement

Vickie, maybe you should put your sweater back on. The V of your thong underwear popping up above your low-rise jeans gives you an unfortunately *cetacean* appearance.

cetacean: belonging to the class of animals that includes whales

Lewis, the way you do the electric slide reminds me of an air-strapped flounder *crangling* along the pier!

crangle: to wriggle and twist

Gold-Digging Bottom Feeders: Your Children's Unfortunate Romantic Choices

Dear Lady Snark,

My wife and I are very concerned about our daughter Jenny. Over spring break, she brought her boyfriend, Ed, home with her from college. Jenny is no beauty and we're sure this guy is just interested in the enormous inheritance she stands to gain when her elderly, childless Uncle Basil passes away (which will be soon). How can I cut him down to size so he'll go away?

Christopher

Chappaqua, New York

My Dear,

How delightful Jenny's uncle sounds—just the sort of man one cannot find in polite society anymore, no matter how hard one tries. Of course, I am happy to share my expertise to assist your family in any way I can.

Foe or Faux?

Test your knowledge of vituperation by determining if the following is an insult or not.

Peggy, have you ever considered that Jerry might have broken off the engagement because of your viraginity?

This is an insult. However, Jerry has not dumped Peggy because she won't put out. He did so because she is a virago: a loud and aggressive woman.

I have extensive experience driving fortune hunters away from my stepchildren. Actually, when I still had some claim on part of Eric's trust fund, I made an art of chasing all suitors away from my stepson. In particular, I tried to explain the advantages of having no heirs to Eric, but the new math has rendered him incapable of calculating how much each extra person living on that trust fund will reduce the amount of his monthly allowance available for video games.

As for you, I am sure there are many unpleasant things you'd enjoy saying to Ed, such as "You money-grubbing gigolo!" or "Get away from my daughter, gold-digging bottom feeder." I know this because of the unfortunate history of my eldest living stepdaughter, Min, which I will relate to you now.

Raised in an overprotective environment by my late husband Bill, Min was an innocent and rather impressionable young woman. In the days when hallucinogenic drugs were widely available at afternoon tea parties, she spent several years in the hazy ambience of a California graduate school. It was there that she became enamored of a young man who called himself "Sirocco" (the first of many warnings that he was unsuitable). Although her father, Bill, had also changed his name (from Wang Su), he did not see this reinvention in the same light.

Nothing Says "I Love You" Like Creative Uses for Feminine Products

During the second year of her Tao of Macramé master's program, Min and her ill wind moved into a "Goddess Yurt" he had built near the Happy Sunshine House commune a few miles from campus. I never visited her there, but Sirocco occasionally made some income penning articles on building "earth-friendly" structures for alternative publications, so I was able to view their home (which appeared to be constructed of recycled sanitary napkins) in a grainy photograph my husband showed me. I never did learn if Min was required to personally provide the building materials as some sort of dowry, though it struck me as likely.

Bill began a futile campaign to blow Sirocco away, as it were. I should note that I was not involved in this effort because of the limited pull I had with Min. For some reason, she was unenthusiastic about having a stepmother her own age and, moreover, believed that I was responsible for her mother's untimely death by poisoned seaweed wrap at a spa the previous year.

Despite my distance from the feud, I know what happened because Min angrily retold most of the stories years later, after her father had been crushed by a falling piano and she came back and claimed what was left of her inheritance to invest in a dot-com startup.

According to my stepdaughter, Bill first sent several threatening letters to Sirocco. (I think it goes without saying that the yurt had no phone.) Sirocco did not read these. The commune, which was their nearest mail stop, considered such correspondence to be group property. Thus, all letters were opened to check for cash and read aloud as a Sunday night entertainment.

The Dark Days of Happy Sunshine House

Min paraphrased her father's invectives, but having perused *The Dark Days of Happy Sunshine House* by Rainbow Butterfly (Singing Flea Press, 1987) I can now share some exact quotes with you, starting with the early letters, in which he used the language of his own social set to criticize Sirocco's lifestyle. I've included translations of his intended meanings, in case they are not clear to you.

Long-haired weirdo!
Translation: That haircut makes you look like a woman, but not as much of a woman as you'll be after I get through with you.

Go hug a tree, you draft-dodging creep.
Translation: If you like nature so much, why don't you go to the jungles of Vietnam, where you are supposed to be anyway, loser!

Given his stunning lack of success, Bill started to adopt the younger generation's terminology in an effort to communicate more clearly.

I'll tell you what I'm going to dig—your grave, hippie boy!
Translation: The only thing I'd appreciate about your existence would be if it ended soon.

My husband's later attempts, as recounted by Ms. Butterfly, were even less successful, often because he tended to confuse the literal with the figurative, as shown below.

I'm going to blow your mind!

While the hippies assumed that Bill was going to reveal some mystery of the cosmos, he was actually referring to the effect his revolver would have on Sirocco's head.

You want to go on a trip?

Needless to say, Min's father was not discussing LSD. The state of altered consciousness he was offering involved a sledgehammer and the trunk of a car.

Keep on trucking! Out of sight!

Finally, what seemed like encouragement to the commune dwellers was actually an offer to pay for the cost of a moving van if Sirocco would pack up his bong collection and go.

In the end, though Bill's efforts did not accomplish his goal, Sirocco's supposed designs on Min's fortune were outwitted by her own devotion to the cause. After hearing about the plight of an ancient redwood tree slated for harvesting, she left the yurt to spend the next six years sitting on a platform (suspended by a macramé sling of her own design) to keep loggers from cutting it down. This action served to end the relationship, since Sirocco was neither athletic nor comfortable with heights.

Having explained the less fruitful course of action to you, I will now tell you what you should say to nip this relationship in the bud. When your daughter is out of the house, try one of these on Ed:

Jenny is so selfless! We still can't believe she signed over her entire anticipated fortune to the kinkajou refuge.

Oh, now that you and our daughter are getting serious, I thought you might like the chance to look over this 1,200-page standard prenuptial agreement you'd have to sign if things went further.

Do you ever get that eerie feeling that someone is watching you? That's the professional sharpshooter I paid to end your relationship.

If the first two don't work, the third is usually "a charm" as my Grandmother Hattie used to say. Do let me know how things work out! And I'd love to meet Jenny's Uncle Basil. I would hate for him to be taken advantage of in this way, and I would even be happy to discuss this matter with him personally over drinks if you wouldn't mind introducing us.

Cordially,

Lady Arabella Snark

Age and Money Before Youth and Silicone

Dear Lady Snark,

I am not sure what to do. My husband and I have been invited to a party this Friday and I am almost sure that his girlfriend, Amy, will be there. I still can't believe he's cheating on me with someone from our own social circle, but it's worse. She's at least ten years younger than I am and very open about the whole thing. When I saw her at the supermarket last week, she told me, "It's just a matter of time!" What on earth can I say if she tries to talk to me?

Genevieve

Lubbock, Texas

My Dear,

It is a law of nature: Ladies of a certain age must learn to fend off the attempts of younger, blonder, firmer women to appropriate their husbands. These naïve girls are apt to look on you as an aging circus tiger that they can poke with a stick for amusement. Their confidence stems from the assumption that you won't maul them in front of an audience, even if they offer you poisoned meat in the form of an announcement that your husband is leaving you.

How foolish these trollops are! You may be old and wrinkly, but, unlike Amy, you know your husband is no prize. Simply acknowledge her statements with a smile and make sure she understands how little they distress you.

Why is this effective? In my experience, there is nothing more off-putting than investing your efforts into a competition only to discover that it wasn't worth winning. When you learn, for example, that the wife of the Greek shipping magnate you thought you were "stealing" is actually encouraging the affair so she'll have more time to shop, a light bulb goes off in your head—except it isn't really a light bulb. It's the blinding glare of the cheap hotel lamp reflecting off his shiny head. In the clear light of that fluorescent bulb, you can see that self-protection is the reason behind his wife's monster shades—not fashion, as you had previously assumed.

But given your position, I'm sure you'd like to see the other side of the coin. Behold Mrs. Jim Ornish, a lady of quality who after years of turning the other cheek in embarrassment has acquired a hardened carapace that no plastic surgeon can take away. At a cocktail party, she encounters her husband's latest fling, Sally, the daughter of her neighbors and former friends, Jack and Mary Slattern. Sally is a vacuous nineteen-year-old who erroneously believes, as Mrs. Ornish once did, that Jim is a "catch."

Sally begins her aggressive display of insecurity by making a backhanded compliment to highlight the obvious disparity between her youth and Mrs. Ornish's "maturity."

> **Sally: Wow, Mrs. Ornish. I haven't seen you since your daughter, you know, used to babysit for me when she was in junior high. You look great for your age!**
>
> **Mrs. Ornish: Thank you, Sally, darling. I wish I could say the same.**

But Sally is still out to make our heroine sweat, so she takes another stab at making Mrs. Ornish feel antiquated.

> **Sally:** Gosh, I love these old-fashioned fireplaces. I suppose when you were younger, you needed them in every room to heat the house, huh?
>
> **Mrs. Ornish:** Don't let your bosoms get too close to the flames, dear. I'm sure Jim would be upset if you let his investments melt.

Undeterred, Sally gets to the point.

> **Sally:** Yeah, I mean, I guess you'll be pretty lonely here next Christmas without your husband.
>
> **Mrs. Ornish:** So true! I'll be here all alone with my trust fund, while you'll have so much company. Perhaps instead of caroling, you can entertain your new companions at the homeless shelter with a reading of the legal agreement that gives me everything if Jim is unfaithful.

Discouraged at her lack of success, Sally plays her trump card.

> **Sally:** I'm sure everything will be different when the baby is born. I hope it's, like, not too weird for you that your son Steve will have a brother twenty-five years younger than him.

Mrs. Ornish: Probably no stranger than it has been with the previous illegitimate offspring my husband has produced. By the way, once you and Jim are married, you can take over the child support for the seven I know of. I'm happy to give you everything I have, Sally! You deserve it.

Remember this lesson and you will glide through life like Hans Brinker on his silver skates, not the cheesy electroplated ones Sally imagines herself wearing when she plunges through the ice into the freezing water of financial doom with Mr. Ornish.

Cordially,

Lady Arabella Snark

Foe or Faux?

Test your knowledge of vituperation by determining if the following is an insult or not.

I do like you, Tony, but Jeb told me you're a bit of a toxophilite.

This is not an insult. Tony enjoys archery.

Test Your Knowledge of Romantic Analogies

In each question, the first pair of words has a logical relationship. Complete the sentence by choosing the word that best completes the second word pair with the same relationship. The first one has been completed for you as an example.

Example: Eve is to apple as my friend Janet is to

    A.   orange

    B.   pomegranate

    C.   mailman

The correct answer is C, mailman. Eve ate an apple in the Garden of Eden because she was tempted by a snake. Janet had an affair with her mailman because her husband is a snake. Now that you can see how simple this is, try a few for yourself!

1.   Elderly millionaire is to supermodel as goldfinch is to

    A.   perch

    B.   sunflowers

    C.   bird-eating spider

2.   Mosquito is to malaria as your husband's Bangkok "business trip" is to

    A.   profits

    B.   success

    C.   gonorrhea

3. Fireplace poker is to head as "you . . ." is to

   A. pronoun

   B. me

   C. ". . . look fat in that dress."

4. Locusts are to crops as your fiancé's stepchildren are to

   A. boarding school

   B. nanny

   C. happiness

5. Wedding is to prenup as Anna Karenina is to

   A. literature

   B. romance

   C. train

6. Plane crash is to pilot error as unattractive bedmate is to

   A. wedding

   B. roses

   C. open bar

Answer key: 1. C; 2. C; 3. C; 4. C; 5. C; 6. C

six. Nah, Nah, Cootie Boy!

In which Timmy learns about RUBBER & GLUE, Betsy discovers that the THESAURUS is a MEGA-DORKY waste of time, & the reader is instructed in PUNS, METAPHORS, and how a contemporary nine-year-old LADY ANNE NEVILLE might reject the unwanted romantic attentions of RICHARD III.

On the Importance of Avoiding Small Plastic Enclosures

It is never too early to learn proper social interaction. The sooner you realize the innate inferiority of other youngsters and learn to deal with them, the better. To my adult readers who feel that children do not need such advice, consider it insurance. They must, after all, last long enough to wrest your former spouse's inheritance from their new siblings so that you may enjoy some of it in your old age.

Admittedly, this is less of an issue for those children who do not stand to inherit anything but a drinking problem. However, all children may be the victims of schoolyard taunts, classroom humiliations, and the horrors of the birthday party.

The problem is that many youngsters have no one to guide them through the unpleasant process of growing up, rather like baby sea turtles. I am familiar with this particular form of marine life because before Amelia's father and I were married, I thought I should appear "maternal" and occasionally volunteered in her fourth grade science class. Thus, perched on the edge of an undersized chair, did I see an instructive nature filmstrip about these endangered little animals, which emerged hopefully from their delicate shells on a remote tropical beach, scrambling happily toward the turquoise waters of the great big ocean.

Of the hundreds of flippered infants to leave the safety of the nest, most suffered ghastly fates: dropped on the rocks to be opened by ravenous seagulls, devoured by giant fishes, or picked up by tourists to endure a Sisyphean struggle, endlessly banging their little heads against the invisible plastic barrier of a cheap aquarium.

That's because their mother was not there to protect them. She left immediately after burying their tiny eggs in the sand, abandoning them for a week of mud baths in Bali.

Foe or Faux?

Test your knowledge of vituperation by determining if the following is an insult or not.

New snow pants, Jeffy? They're totally stridulent!

This is an insult. The speaker wishes to ridicule the shrill sounds caused by Jeffy's puffy nylon-encased legs rubbing together.

If you are a young person reading this now, perhaps it sounds familiar. While your mother is off at the spa balancing her energy fields with a full body mango scrub, you are being brought up by an eighteen-year-old nanny who cannot speak English and came to take care of you because she thought it would be "fun." Now that she has arrived, discovered no one within a thousand miles speaks Swedish, and learned that your parents do not intend to let her drive the car except when you are in it, your chances of getting the advice that will keep you out of a plastic aquarium are slim.

On the other hand, if you are a young person reading this, you are already blessed with above-average reading skills. Though that is not much of an advantage at recess, it reminds me of Amelia, who spent much of her childhood running away from stocky girls waving field hockey sticks. It is thus with compassion that I offer you some suggestions on playground survival—not just because my attorney told me it would look better to the judge if I appeared to care about children whose trust funds I can't touch.

Liar, Liar, Pants on Fire! Verbal Techniques in Self Defense

Dear Lady Snark,

This boy Eddie is really mean to me. I was at recess yesterday and he came up to me and started calling me "booger boy." I said, "Am not!" but he just kept saying, "Are too!" Then he started repeating everything

I said. It made me really mad. Then he broke my glasses, kicked me in the shins, and knocked me down. And then he sat on me and twisted my arm really hard and made fart noises and told everybody they came from me. What can I do if he tries to do that tomorrow? I want to call him something really bad, but I don't know the right word.

Timmy

Sandusky, Ohio

My Dear,

I believe the term you are searching for is *sociopath*. But though Eddie may be familiar with this word from his many long meetings with counselors and tough-love summer camps, he will not see this as "bad" and is more likely to bask happily in the fear it arouses in parents, teachers, and clergymen.

As you discovered, "am not" is not very useful in verbal self-defense. The limited exchange that follows such a rejoinder can go on ad nauseum until an adult intervenes or, more likely, the accused bursts into tears. It is also ineffective to

cry out, "Liar, liar, pants on fire!" As Queen Gertrude observed to her son Hamlet, the louder such a protest is shouted, the less convincing it sounds.

For this reason, as difficult as you will find it, you must not let anyone know that you are upset about any pants-wetting comments they might make; nor should you rise to the bait when it is suggested that your dog is less intelligent than a cardboard box.

I realize this kind of composure is difficult to attain. I myself spent three years practicing the art of equanimity on the island of Muu Xu with the solitary Master Lo after my yacht was taken by pirates in the South Seas, but I still find myself wanting to eviscerate inept shampoo girls with a nail file from time to time. However, I have confidence in you to overcome your crybaby tendencies. And once you do, you should memorize a powerful comeback, as shown below:

> **Eddie: Fartbag!**
>
> **Timmy: I know you are, but what am I?**

This magical phrase easily reflects the insult back onto the speaker with the power of a secret weapon from a James Bond movie. Flummoxed, the original attacker is now on the defensive, relegated to desperate

"Am nots!" until their ultimate dissolution into hysteria, their fate now sealed by your chess-like strategy. Similarly, you can use this more poetic version:

> **Eddie: Pea brain!**
>
> **Timmy: I'm rubber and you're glue. Whatever you say bounces off of me and sticks to you!**

Some might suggest this alternate defense:

> **Eddie: Poopy pants!**
>
> **Timmy: It takes one to know one.**

However, this has the disadvantage of being an admission; you might find that instead of scoring a point with your peers, you and Eddie will both be given a wide berth when it is time to choose partners for the Cinderella dance.

I must be honest, though, and tell you that I do not believe you will have much luck with words in your Eddie-related dealings. As useful as these parries might be with your other classmates, you would be better off simply hiding until he is sent to military school. As this exile will likely be triggered by an altercation gone wrong, keeping your distance now will ensure that your freedom does not come at the expense of one of your eyes or fingers.

Cordially,

Lady Arabella Snark

Malediction 101: Chalk—The Other White Meat

Sometimes it is safer to confuse kids who are mean to you than to insult them directly. The following cruel words for your classmate's unsavory dietary habits are most appropriate for bullies; since they will not understand any of them, they are less likely to beat you up upon hearing them.

You know, Billy, your abnormal *esurience* makes me wonder if you might be playing host to a parasitic flatworm.
esurience: hunger

Of course, I hesitate to say that you are *vermivorous*, though it might be true based on what I have seen of your nutritional sensibility.
vermivorous: worm eating

After all, your evident *pica* problem has resulted in the disappearance of all our classroom chalk and a number of figures from the play farm, including a small metal tractor.

pica: an unnatural desire to eat things that are not food

Plus, in the three months we've been in class together, I've never seen you perform *ablutions*.

ablutions: the act of washing oneself

On the other hand, I've noticed you kissing your dog Spot on several occasions. Since Spot is a well-known *coprophagist*, that would make for a more direct opportunity to ingest a parasite.

coprophagist: one who eats feces

Make Like the Wind and Blow: Disposing of Unwanted Companions

Dear Lady Snark,

My brother always wants to hang out with my friends and me but he's only seven and he acts like a baby. I'm ten and I don't know why my mom keeps making me play with him. It's really embarrassing. What can I say to make him go away?

Brian

Smelterville, Idaho

My Dear,

I note that you did not specify whether you wish his disappearance to be permanent or temporary. How cunning of you! One should never put such requests in writing.

As evinced by your missive, the relationship between younger and older siblings, unlike the quality of mercy, is strained. This tension is sometimes enough to make older brothers and sisters employ rat poison, pillows, or carefully sharpened pencils in an effort to permanently eradicate the scourge of attention-gettingly cute babies. Once these interlopers learn to walk, there is no fail-safe comment that will drive them from your otherwise entertaining play dates, but I do have a few suggestions, starting with:

" Why don't you go play in traffic?

Of course, you can explain later that you meant it figuratively. There are many variations on this theme, most of them involving puns, such as:

> **Why don't you make like a banana and split?**

In addition to making your aggravation with his company clear, this shows off a certain verbal flair that will no doubt impress your companions—once they have figured out the joke themselves. If they are not terribly sharp, you might have to explain the double meaning of "split" to them.

It is possible that you will get carried away and wish to use more creative (and aggressive) versions, such as:

> **Why don't you make like milk and expire?**
>
> **Why don't you make like a coat and hang?**
>
> **Why don't you make like bacon and fry?**

However, the obvious flaw in these more complex statements is that they will probably go over your brother's head. To ensure success, you might have to lower yourself to a simple "Get lost!" or a hit man.

Cordially,

Lady Arabella Snark

James Joyce Runs Like a Girl!

Dear Lady Snake,

I heard about you from my mother, Fernanda Esmeralda Mendoza Herrera. Maybe you remember her because you both used to like Señor Aaron Baker at the same time. My mother says you are not nice and can say mean things very well, so I want to ask you about my problem. We are in New York now and Ricky, who is one of the boys in my class, always says mean things to me. So last week, when we played softball, I said, "You have buttered fingers!" but he laughed. So I hit him because he is short and weak like a girl, he cannot fight, but then I must stay inside for recess. What should I say to him?

Miguel

New York, New York

My Dear,

On the playground, the resourceful take their cues from The Lord of the Flies. If you have not read that children's classic, it is about a group of bright, energetic young boys who camp on a remote island and learn to do outdoorsy things, like make fire using a pair of spectacles and the sun. As this turns out to be unfortunate for the myopic youngster who was originally wearing them, the moral of the story is that if you are short, weak like a girl, and cannot fight, you are better off with extended wear contact lenses.

For you, this means that you should highlight Ricky's mental, social, and physical weaknesses in a public forum so that he will feel ridiculed and cry. For instance, you might point out to the other children that he runs like a girl. However, given your previous mistake (it should be butterfingers, not buttered fingers) I think you need a primer on avoiding common errors made by inexperienced taunters.

Such small changes in delivery can turn your explosive Molotov cocktail into a harmlessly sweet Shirley Temple, so use care when directing such remarks at other classmates and remember that audience is of paramount importance in gender related-criticisms. Stating the obvious will get you nowhere.

❝❝ Miguel: You run like a girl.

Beth: And your point is?

Likewise, the pain and injury such caustic comments can produce depends on the unequal power relationship between the sexes and therefore will not work in reverse.

❝❝ Miguel: You run like a boy.

Beth: Thank you.

Intelligence is another rich area for criticism. For example, the following insult works because it exploits the irony of Sookey's taxonomic confusion:

> **Sookey, you're so dumb you named your dog "Miss Kitty"!**

Stupidity is not the only mental condition you can criticize, though; for children, a surplus of intelligence can be as undesirable as a deficit, as my stepdaughter Amelia learned the hard way. However, keep in mind that students who are culturally rewarded for academic success will be unfazed by your mockery.

> **Miguel: You're the biggest board-erasing eggheaded megabrain in the third grade!**
>
> **Hyun Jung: Laugh while you can, dorkball! I was just offered a full academic scholarship to MIT.**

In addition, when using metaphors and similes to critique appearance, try to make comparisons that will be easily understood and avoid those that require encyclopedic knowledge on the part of your interlocutor. Taking the opportunity to show off your expertise in veterinary medicine or Irish literature will be a waste of time with less informed classmates.

Wrong: You look like a manatee with hypothyroidism.

Right: Blubber!

Wrong: I'm sorry, but if you're going for that James Joyce–circa–*Finnegans Wake* look, you totally missed the mark.

Right: Four-eyes!

Even when making base accusations about objectionable bathroom habits, stay away from allusions to any cultural artifacts that could be unfamiliar:

Wrong: What's the difference between Ricky's pee and Prince Albert? Prince Albert is in the can!

If you want to be creative in a way that will be appreciated by your infantile peers, try a parody of something they are certain to know:

> **You tinkled, tinkled on your shoe! Oh how I wonder, where's your poo?**

I hope this has been of assistance. And by the way, I remember your mother well. I do hope her scars have healed sufficiently that she can model again. As I told the authorities at the time, I truly believed that the bottle contained eau de cologne and not battery acid.

Cordially,

Lady Arabella Snark

Foe or Faux?

Test your knowledge of vituperation by determining if the following is an insult or not.

Gee, Mimi, I really had to admire your mendacity when Mrs. Estevez asked what happened to our class guinea pig.

This may or may not be an insult, depending on the speaker's attachment to the guinea pig. Mendacity is lying.

Supersize Me! Enhancing Your Limited Vocabulary

Dear Lady Snark,

There's this girl Celia in my school who is so dumb. She is like the dumbest girl in second grade. She is always eating paste and stuff. So last week I got in a fight with her and I called her a dork lots of times. I told my sister Cathy about it and she said I should learn more words instead of always using the same one. Cathy is in high school so she is really smart but you are really old, so maybe you are smarter. Do I need to know lots of words for fights?

Betsy

Crowheart, Wyoming

My Dear,

As you probably believe twenty to be "really old," I will overlook the aspersions you have cast on my nubility. And the answer to your question is no, but your sister's mistake is understandable. She is probably learning in her English Composition classes that using the word "dork" fifty times in an essay is "bad." However, you do not need to acquire a vast and sophisticated vocabulary for verbal altercations on the playground, nor should you. Whatever your sister tells you, this rule about scouring the thesaurus for synonyms does not apply to children; simplicity and repetition make for more potent slurs when speaking to your pint-sized peers.

Still, if you feel that not knowing enough words is keeping your insults from having the strong emotional impact you'd like, simply add a few prefixes to the four or five insults you know for an exponential increase in hatefulness. You may also increase your word power by creating compound nouns (e.g., dork + ball) or intensify the meaning with a suffix, such as –azoid, as demonstrated by this argument between Jimmy and Freddy.

Jimmy: You are a dork!

Freddy: You are a super-dork!

Jimmy: Oh, yeah? Well, you are a super-duper-dork!

Freddy: Extra-super-duper-dorkball!

Jimmy: Ultra-extra-super-duper-dorkhead!

Freddy: Mega-ultra-extra-super-duper-dorkbrain!

Jimmy: Giganto-mega-ultra-extra-super-duper-dorkazoid!

Freddy: Humunga-giganto-mega-ultra-extra-super-duper-dorkasaurus!

As for fancy synonyms, you can worry about those when you are an adult, though if my old cellmate Tabitha is to be believed, carrying a weapon eliminates the need for a large vocabulary even after you are old enough to drive a getaway car.

Cordially,

Lady Arabella Snark

Foe or Faux?

Test your knowledge of vituperation by determining if the following is an insult or not.

So, Lulu, has anyone said anything to you about your constant propinquity to Miss Elfland?

This is an insult. That Lulu spends her time close to Miss Elfland reveals her desire to be the teacher's pet.

The Adventures of Cootie Boy!

Dear Lady Snark,

I love books! When I grow up, I am going to study all the time and then I'm going to be a writer like you! My problem is when I try to say bad things about the other kids in a good way, they don't get it. Like yesterday, I fell down on the playground and cried and Mike B. told me I was a baby. So I said, "Oh, yeah? Well, at least I don't have an unhealthy fascination with the mucous expelled from my nasal cavities!" He just looked at me funny. How come that didn't work?

Pauley

Omaha, Nebraska

My Dear,

This is the price you pay for being a passionate academic. Now, you make the mistake wasting your advanced vocabulary on other children. Fifteen years from now, you will spend a decade researching the bathroom habits of Edith Wharton, only to discover that someone else has beaten you to publication with the definitive book on the subject. I keep trying to explain the futility of such a course to Amelia, but she still spent last summer comparing early and late Victorian wallpaper for a professor in Women's Studies and was unmoved by my suggestion that her time would be better employed stripping the hideous Victorian wallpaper in the ballroom at Elfingrot Manor. Eric didn't want to do it either, so I suppose I will have to hire someone.

My first advice to you is to stop now and save yourself the price of a small private island in tuition. As for your immediate problem, you should take care to use simple language when speaking with your peers when you want them to understand you. Your example contains too many big words.

> **Wrong:** Oh, yeah? Well, at least I don't have an unhealthy fascination with the mucous expelled from my nasal cavities!

The superior comeback is far more succinct:

> **Right:** Booger!

Below are more practical examples of how to simplify your speech for maximum-strength assaults.

> **Wrong:** Your birth was an unplanned event that has caused your parents years of tooth-gnashing regret.

> **Right:** You were a mistake!

Wrong: Your trust fund is so poorly managed that when you graduate from high school, you'll have no choice but to enroll in a shabby public university with other peons. A few pennies won't help you, so you may as well donate them to a worthy cause.

Right: Give me your milk money or I'll beat the poop out of you!

Wrong: I believe your real objection to breaking into our neighbor's garage is not your superior morals, but a fear of legal authority and the threat of your parents curtailing your social privileges.

Right: Fraidy cat!

Wrong: Your personal hygiene is lacking to a degree that invites parasites to take up residence on your person.

Right: Cootie boy!

Library books also make for good attacks if words fail you. I hope you'll take my advice, but if you continue on this misguided path, don't come running to me when you can't pay your student loans. I am saving up for some new martini glasses and a yacht to put them in.

Cordially,

Lady Arabella Snark

The Quixotic *Quiz*

Test Your Knowledge of Puerile Remarks

Because of budget cuts, the Ada Lovelace School for Gifted Children has been shut down. Nine-year-old Lovelace alum Gregory Entemann (whose IQ, as he likes to tell people, can be expressed as the product of his age squared, multiplied by 1.89) is now about to become the most unpopular child in his fourth-grade class at the James K. Polk Elementary School.

Gregory: Polk was a fool! His handling of the Mexican-American War was an embarrassment to the thirty states that made up the union at that time.

Frieda: I'll poke a fool!

Dodging Frieda's index finger, Gregory formulates a retort. Unfortunately, his focus in school up to this point has been the plays of Shakespeare. As previously mentioned, these are more likely to make adults laugh than cry; they have even less impact on uncomprehending children. Help Gregory to find the age-appropriate insult by matching each mistakenly scholarly choice on the left to the superior immature response on the right.

1.____ Hoy day, what a sweep of vanity comes this way!

A.   You smell, fartbag.

2.____ Even like a fawning greyhound in the leash.

B.   Bigmouth scaredy cat!

3.____ Not so much brain as ear wax.

C.   You're stuck up!

continued

4.___ Foul-spoken coward, that thund'rest with thy tongue, and with thy weapon nothing dar'st perform.

D.   Jerkazoid.

5.___ Thou odoriferous stench! Sound rottenness!

E.   You're gross. Beat it, icky-poo!

6.___ Out, dunghill!

F.   Megadork.

7.___ Most impenetrable cur that ever kept with men.

G.   Get lost, poopy pants.

8.___ Never hung poison on a fouler toad. Out of my sight! Thou dost infect my eyes.

H.   Teacher's pet!

Answer Key: 1. C; 2. H; 3. F; 4. B; 5. A; 6. G; 7. D; 8. E

seven. Your Family: You Can't Live with Them; You Can't Live Without Their Money

In which we study how EUPHEMISMS & POLITE BEHAVIOR can spoil an otherwise lovely evening; why THE TOWN PUMP is not actually a good place to get your drinking water; & how a GREEN MAMBA can help you pay off your credit cards, but will not necessarily stop all of your RELATIVES from following you to THE ENDS OF THE EARTH.

Bob's Your Uncle, Unfortunately

Between the time your elderly relatives begin to irritate you at the age of two and the time they kick the bucket is a very long time indeed. Doesn't it seem that if only smelly Uncle Julius could transfer that trust now instead of giving you a ten dollar bill every year in your birthday card, the world would be a better place?

If you are young and still living at home, you probably think that you're getting the worst of your relatives now. After all, you cannot attend a single family gathering without being brutally pinched and infantilized by Uncle Julius and his ilk, none of whom will ever shrivel up quite enough to actually die.

You are mistaken; the worst is yet to come. As soon as you are old enough to sit at the big people's table, you will be expected to provide that table at your very own house, while your devious siblings find ways to avoid hosting these familial horror shows.

Every grandparent, sibling, and cousin will have an excuse, too, but none of them will ever be too busy to come to your house for the holidays and crush chocolate-covered cherries into your carpet while they complain that Grandma never used canned onions in the green bean casserole.

"Why don't I just move to Australia?" you might ask yourself.

You can try, but you will be sorely disappointed. The fact that your little seaside cottage in Wollongong has no spare bedroom will in no way protect you from the onslaught of second cousins twice removed who will descend upon your home like a horde of locusts—all of whom will guarantee that you will not even notice they are there and none of whom will be nearly as unobtrusive as a kangaroo in a Mini Cooper.

Foe or Faux?

Test your knowledge of vituperation by determining if the following is an insult or not.

As much as you try to hide it, we all know it's been a while since you stopped being dentigerous, Granny. Why don't you have some mashed potatoes?

This is an insult. To be dentigerous is to have teeth.

And, much like locusts, they will devour your crops and deplete your stores of food over and over again, until every grain in your last amphora has been consumed and the clerk at the local market realizes it is in poor taste to make further jokes about them voraciously licking the counters until the finish has been removed. Once proved true, such jests are no longer amusing.

I suppose I should admit that I don't have this problem myself, because I wrote a form letter to all my relatives in 1969 explaining that I had contracted a rare, slow-acting but highly contagious kind of leprosy in France. My relatives are remarkably gullible.

If yours are not, you really only have three choices: You can insult them and forget about the inheritance, learn to deal with them and hope for the money, or figure out an ingenious way to turn the will in your favor only hours before they die in a mysterious accident. Feel free to contact me privately to discuss fees if you are interested in the third option. Otherwise, tips on the first two are provided in this chapter.

Problems with Ingrained Politeness: Would You Mind Fucking Yourself?

Dear Lady Snark,

I've been having a lot of problems with my mother-in-law since my wife Melanie and I moved back to the states from Afghanistan, where we were working for a relief agency. For example, she says things like, "All those cookies I made just for you seem to have been eaten, Melanie, but you're still so thin!" and "How interesting that the yard hasn't been mowed." She always says she's a passive person, but it feels like she's attacking me. Still, unless she comes right out and says something, I don't feel comfortable defending myself. Can you give me some advice?

Drew

Los Angeles, California

My Dear,

Your passive-aggressive mother-in-law is pretending to have confused the passive voice with passivity. However, she has no such misunderstanding about the two; she is just taking advantage of your "pleasant" (read: doormat-like) nature.

Perhaps her complaint is that her daughter went all the way to Afghanistan and all she got for a son-in-law was a penniless do-gooder in a lousy T-shirt, when Melanie could have married a Taliban drug lord instead, providing the family with an endless river of cash.

While there is nothing I can do about that, I can help you with your communication problem, namely that you apparently believe telling another human being to "go fuck him- or herself" is somehow less than genteel.

Nothing could be further from the truth. Charmingly polite responses to affronts may sound "cultured" or "refined" to uneducated ears, but they will also allow others to trample over your feelings like polo ponies over an heirloom Aubusson rug.

To be truly assertive, you must give up the misguided notion that the strongest feelings must be couched in indirect language. Overt malevolence is far more effective and far likelier to earn you the respect you deserve.

The first order of business is to discard passivity—and I don't mean the grammatical kind. You may have deluded yourself into believing that you can use polite phrases and be forthright at the same time, but you can't. Your mother-in-law will ignore your subtle remarks with the same skill she uses to avoid seeing the tip jar at her nail salon.

Let's look at an example of someone suffering from the same affliction. In Bridgeport, Connecticut, twenty-six-year-old Emily is playing hostess to Bob and Sue Eckhart for the first time since her marriage to their son John. The Eckharts own a large and profitable salmon-canning factory in Alaska, but are not listed on the social register, nor will they ever be. They have also made it clear that with the exception of a small trust, the bulk of their fortune will go to their other son Mike, who for some inexplicable reason enjoys living in Alaska and canning salmon.

Foe or Faux?

Test your knowledge of vituperation by determining if the following is an insult or not.

Oh, Cousin Jeanette, seeing all those hours of slides from your trip makes me agree that you should go back to France as soon as possible. Maybe you could stay in an oubliette next time!

This is an insult. An oubliette (from the French word for forget) is a prison cell under the floor, usually in a castle. The speaker would like Aunt Jeanette and her slide projector to be tossed into one and "forgotten," even as her agonized screams drown out otherwise pleasant dinner party conversation.

While in the kitchen, Emily's mother-in-law hovers over her, making critical comments about her "newfangled" low-fat cooking. If Emily follows her natural instinct to be "polite," she will probably respond by asking Sue for John's favorite recipes, all the while burning with the rage of one thousand fat girls not invited to dance at cotillion.

She might fool herself into thinking that delivering her message with a raised eyebrow will cancel out the obsequiousness of her request. It will not. Irony cannot shift the balance of power, as mothers-in-law are notoriously impervious to indirect hostility. And she could try using a stronger version:

 I'm sorry, Sue. Perhaps I should have asked for your recipes so that I could more effectively clog my husband's arteries and kill him, leaving me an impoverished widow living pathetically in your spare bedroom.

But this is unlikely to have the desired effect. It is more probable that Sue, recognizing Emily's insecurity, will gleefully martyr herself and offer to cook "real food" that "sticks to your ribs" for the remainder of her stay.

Unfortunately, even if she has mastered the vocabulary, Emily, like you, may be confounded by her early training in "manners."

 I'm sorry, Sue. If it's not too much trouble, would you mind fucking yourself?

With such a weak effort, Emily shows that she does not possess a spine, but merely a back brace supporting her invertebrate torso. After this rejoinder, Sue will pity her, but still feel compelled to destroy her marriage as quickly as possible. And most likely, she will succeed.

Emily must learn the subtle distinction between assertive language (what she says) and impolite language (what other people say). Once she understands her proper place in the world, she will be able to speak confidently and directly.

 Listen you fat cow, if I wanted my husband to be a blimp like yours, I would feed him salted lard for breakfast. Why don't you go back to Alaska and get eaten by a bear?

Note that Emily uses the passive voice ("get eaten") without being passive. Her meaning is clear, despite the indirect construction. If you are unable to do the same, you might consider moving to a safer location, like the mouth of a volcano.

Cordially,

Lady Arabella Snark

Don't Ask if You Don't Want to Know

Dear Lady Snark,

I'm going home for the holidays next weekend and all my relatives are going to be there, asking me the same stupid, rude questions they asked me the last time, like "Don't you think you'd look prettier if you lost weight?" It makes me so mad. Is there any way I can answer a question like that without being rude?

Juanita

Bent Spoon, Colorado

My Dear,

Probably, but why bother? If you answer inappropriate questions with even more inappropriate answers, you'll have the pleasure of watching your relatives nervously scurry off to hide from you behind the Christmas tree like so many cockroaches behind the fridge. Before you go, just be sure to fortify yourself with a quart of brandy and memorize these perfect retorts to the top ten obnoxious family questions.

1. **Don't you think you'd look prettier if you lost weight?**
    Yes, but then it would be more difficult to crush you.

2. **Your pumpkin pie isn't as good as Mom's. What's that weird taste?**
    Arsenic.

3. **Why aren't you married?**
    I guess I'm just afraid of settling, the way Uncle Milton did with you.

4. **When are you going to have a baby?**
    Didn't Mom ever tell you I was born a boy?

5. **Are you still paying back those student loans?**
    Actually, the government just writes them off if you drop out of college to become a junkie.

6. **Don't you want to pull my finger?**
    Not unless I can take it all the way off.

7. **Why are you still at that dead-end job?**
    I guess they haven't noticed the embezzling yet.

8. **Why do you allow your son Timmy to watch so much television? Don't you know how bad that is for a child?**
    It's the only thing that keeps him away from the knives.

9.   Why do you wear so much makeup?

It's a professional requirement for my job as a harlot.

10.   Since you're only twenty-three, I can get you a great deal on some life insurance! What do you say?

I don't think I'd qualify. I'm planning to commit suicide after dessert.

Happy Holidays!

Cordially,

Lady Arabella Snark

I Wish You Would Pass Away, You Pleasingly Plump, Mentally Challenged Person!

Dear Lady Snark,

When I was growing up, my mother told me that you shouldn't say bad things directly. Like if someone has a really ugly new painting, you should say it's "interesting" or if they are insane, you should say they are "different." But sometimes when I'm talking to someone who really pisses me off, like my mom's cousin Neeley, those expressions seem kind of lame.

She loves to make digs about my grades and my love life when we visit and she's even trained her pet parrot Bart to do the same. She is sure I won't retaliate directly because my mom is standing right there, giving me the "just be nice" look. You're about the same age, so maybe my mom will listen to you. Would you give me permission to say something stronger the next time Bart asks me why I don't have a girlfriend, or do you agree with her?

Keith

Baton Rouge, Louisiana

My Dear,

I believe Cher and Kim Jong Il are about the same age, but I don't think you're likely to spot Mr. Il sporting a sequined Bob Mackey g-string anytime soon. Those revoltingly "kind" expressions you describe are called euphemisms, but I have another word for that kind of talk: pathetic. For example, as a "polite" person, when encountering the recently bereaved Mr. Binghamton at the dry cleaners, you may feel that you ought to say:

66 **Mark, I was so sorry to hear about your loss. In spite of all the difficulties you had and the fact that Camille's condition**

157

" was longstanding, it still must have been a terrible shock for you. Please accept my heartfelt condolences and let me know if there is anything I can do to help ease your pain.

when what you really mean is:

" Mark, I can't tell you what a relief it is for all of us that your mother-in-law finally bit the dust. That old shrew routinely ran over our mailboxes and family pets every time she was on a drunk, and I'm sure you've been waiting for the day since she publicly emasculated you at Sandra's anniversary party. If I were you, I'd be ecstatic to be free. Let's go out and celebrate.

Although polite expressions have their place (for example, when speaking to older relatives who have named you in their will), they seriously undercut the impact of assertive language. A few typical mistakes involving euphemisms follow, with suggestions for more forceful wording.

Wrong: How do you look? Well, Lillian, I suppose that red sweater is a bit snug.

Right: You're right, Lillian, that red sweater does look very European. Kind of like a stack of Gouda cheeses I saw on my last holiday in Switzerland.

Wrong: So Susan, I heard that Trip has taken on a tremendous amount of charity work this year. It's wonderful that he can devote so much time to helping his fellow man.

Right: You must have a fantastic lawyer to have kept Trip out of prison after that debacle with the anaconda and the drunken sorority pledges. How many hours of community service did he get?

Wrong: No, Amanda won't be going to St. Cecily's this year. I'm afraid she isn't quite cut from the same cloth as your daughter Carolyn.

Right: No, Amanda didn't get into St. Cecily's. But after seeing what a bull-dyke Carolyn turned into after four years of single-sex education, we think it's for the best.

Wrong: I'm sorry, but I believe your car is not exactly in the right spot. If you look closely, you'll see my name on the plate there.

Right: Move your car out of my reserved space, bitch, or I'll rip the chain off your designer bag and choke you with it.

I hope this will help you to have a more enjoyable time on your next visit with your "interesting" and "different" relative. Should your mother faint from the shock, perhaps the talkative Bart can be of assistance. I have heard that burnt feathers are excellent for reviving unconscious persons.

Cordially,

Lady Arabella Snark

Foe or Faux?

Test your knowledge of vituperation by determining if the following is an insult or not.

Sadie, I'd visit more often, but you know you and Mitch have been way too orgulous since you bought that expensive new house!

This is an insult. Sadie and Mitch are too proud of their fancy new residence.

An Archaic Metaphor for Promiscuous Young Women That Involves the Communal Water Supply

Dear Lady Snark,

I don't really get along with my Great Aunt Sylvia, who is about a hundred years old. The way she talks to me sounds kind of nasty, but I don't always get what she is trying to say. Like last week, we had to go visit her in the rest home (my mom thinks we're going to get some money out of her) and my brother told her that I went to Cancun with my boyfriend, Harry, over spring break. Great Aunt Sylvia said, "I thought you were seeing Carl. How many does that make this year? Pretty soon, those college boys will call you the town pump!" I'm sure that's bad, but I don't know what it means. Do you?

Chelsea

Bear's Neck, Arkansas

My Dear,

What it means is that you are less likely to see that inheritance money than your brother. But to answer your real question, having been married to a couple of superannuated gentlemen, I am naturally conversant with many insults of antiquity.

As you say, the first step in dealing with the barbs of an older relative is to understand what he or she is trying to express. Even if they seem quaint today, it is important to remember that these sayings were at one time flaming arrows of nastiness; that is certainly how they are meant by your great aunt.

Let us begin with the town pump. To understand this metaphor, you must first get a handle, so to speak, on the primitive plumbing of your great aunt's youth. Back when she suffered ten mile walks through the snow wearing three corsets and a chastity belt made of cast iron to get to classes at the one-room schoolhouse, everyone got their water from a central pump in the center of town.

Thus do you, in your great aunt's imagination, sit in the center of campus providing your hot, wet favors to all comers who do not yet have indoor plumbing. In other words, she believes you to be a skeezy slut. In preparation for future conversations, I offer some translations for other antiquated expressions she might use:

Tramp: This word is essentially the same as the town pump, with the difference that you wander from place to place offering your erotic services to various men while carrying your belongings in a bandana on the end of a stick.

Nogoodnik: You might think this term for an essentially bad person, like the cans of beans Aunt Sylvia has been serving you from her bomb shelter since your childhood, dates from the 1950s. You'd be wrong; they both made their debut in the thirties. Bon appétit!

Pansy: This one is for your brother. Great Aunt Sylvia is trying to let him know that he just isn't masculine enough. This insult could be triggered by his wearing a pink shirt or demonstrating a general disinclination to do yard work or date the town pump.

Longhair: In the old days, when Great Aunt Sylvia had just retired, wearing your hair below the collar made you a part of the counterculture. Having lived, like her sofa, encased in plastic for the last twenty-five years, she is unaware that most hippies are now middle-aged accountants whose idea of radicalism is to buy an overpriced head of organic lettuce once a month.

Whippersnapper: You think you're hot, but as far as Great Aunt Sylvia is concerned, you're not! Insolent little pissant.

Pissant: Great Aunt Sylvia wants to demonstrate how insignificant you are, just like a tiny insect. Try crawling up her leg and see what she says then.

But seriously, how should you respond to these comments? If you are still holding out hopes for an inheritance, the recommended response to all of these negative assessments is, "Thank you for your candor, Great Aunt Sylvia! I am trying to do my best to live up to the marvelous example you've set, despite the horrific chafing brought on by this cast iron chastity-belt." And you should really visit more often so that you can change her opinion of you. Just make sure not to bring your brother with you. He sounds like a troublemaker.

Cordially,

Lady Arabella Snark

Malediction 101: How to Get Yourself Written out of a Will

Normally, you'd like to stay in the good graces of those in a position to leave you an inheritance. However, if the inheritance consists of a substantial newspaper collection or the remainder of Great Aunt Sylvia's bomb shelter provisions, you might not mind causing a little antagonism. Here are some choice words to use as you relinquish your claim.

Tell us about your girlhood in the *antediluvian* days, Great Aunt Cookie! Like, which of Noah's sons did you think was cuter: Shem or Japheth?
antediluvian: during the time before the Biblical flood

Oh, did you notice my involuntary *horripilation*, Grandpa? I assure you it wasn't a reaction to your unfortunate colostomy bag story. I was just startled when I accidentally brushed against the patchy fluff on your mole and thought a centipede was crawling up my arm.
horripilation: the standing up of hairs on the body or head

Aunt Olive, no matter what anyone says, I think the *rugosity* of your face is as majestic as the Grand Canyon!
rugosity: state of being wrinkled

Uncle Dexter, is your yappy little Yorkie still missing? After he'd bitten me for the third time this morning, I *defenestrated* him from the guest room, but I feel sure he'll be back soon.

defenestrate: throw out a window

Yes, Grandma, it is amazing how young you look! People would probably still think you were twenty if it weren't for your shrunken posture, gray hair, powdery skin, and *lanate* chin.

lanate: wooly

The Quixotic *Quiz*

Test Your Knowledge of Locomotion and Exotic Poisons

. . . .

Part 1. Two trains are coming toward each other on the same track. Train A, which is carrying your mother-in-law, leaves Station 1 at 10:34 AM and travels at a speed of 93 miles per hour. After Train A has traveled for 61 miles, it stops for 7 minutes and 15 seconds to avoid hitting a cow and when it starts traveling again, it takes 5 minutes to get up to its original speed. Then, for 14 minutes, a large bird sits on top of the caboose and slows the train's pace by 3 percent. Train B leaves Station 2 at 10:45 A.M. and travels for 22 miles at 75 miles per hour, then speeds up and travels the remainder of the distance at 130 miles per hour. The total distance between Station 1 and Station 2 is 540 miles. At what time will the two trains crash?

A. 12:47 P.M.

B. 1:03 P.M.

C. Not soon enough

Part 2. If you have foolishly invited some of your wealthy, elderly relatives to your home for Christmas, you may find yourself wishing they would "depart." Below is a variety of items one might place around the house to speed up an inheritance. See if you can match each recommended toxin with the ideal spot to put it. (Please note that this material is provided for informational purposes only. You should never actually use or even possess any of these items, not only because you will certainly get caught, but also because, according to my parole officer, it is wrong to kill people.)

continued

Inheritance accelerator	Most effective if placed in
1. ___ green mamba	A. almond marzipan
2. ___ cyanide	B. an open fire
3. ___ scorpion fish	C. conveniently locked garage
4. ___ deadly lawn galerina mushroom	D. Christmas tree
5. ___ carbon monoxide	E. coat closet
6. ___ Gila monster	F. stuffing
7. ___ horse chestnuts	G. bathtub

Answer Key: Part 1. C; Part 2. 1. D; 2. A; 3. G; 4. F; 5. C; 6. E; 7. B.

eight. Real Men Don't Wear Gold Lamé

In which we examine the lives & manners of GENTLEMEN and learn that some, to our SHOCK & DISMAY, are partial to STRETCH VELVET & oblivious to irony; some host BLANKET PARTIES & carry a BANGER; others take the road less traveled, only to find that they would have been better off staying at home listening to GILBERT & SULLIVAN.

169

The Bell Tolls for King Cottonmouth

Perhaps you think it is unusual that I have devoted an entire chapter of this book to men, imagining that they can take care of themselves and do not need my help.

Not so. If men were truly resilient, all my husbands would still be alive.

Fragile mortality is a problem for all men, not just those I have married. Poor manners in traffic, at the golf course, or even in the supermarket can lead to death (or at the very least, personal injury). While women have clear-cut rules, so that one knows which behavior will provoke a snub or a poisoned éclair, men's relationships have become increasingly less defined over the years as the concept of masculinity has eroded.

I blame this on the professional wrestling television programs my stepson Eric so enjoys. If you have not witnessed such a spectacle, I envy you. However, I must describe it for you to fully understand how very, very confused our notions of what makes a man have become.

The competitors are generally large, smooth skinned, and poured into the sort of shiny stretch unitards normally seen on women in vintage aerobics videos. After shouting their strategies at the announcer, the wrestlers gaze deeply into one another's eyes from a distance of approximately two inches.

"You're *mine*, Hematite! You're going *down*!" proclaims King Cottonmouth, tossing his flowing, bleached locks over a well-oiled shoulder.

"No way!" retorts his rival, carefully adjusting his designer sunglasses, "*I'm* going to take *you*."

This "who's on top" banter continues until one wrestler (who has slyly gone to hide behind a chair) leaps upon his rival with an animal cry. The pair then proceeds to create a series of tableaux that appear to be from the *Kama Sutra*, Vatsyayana's ancient Indian textbook of carnal satisfaction. Occasionally, the tension is broken by a wrestler who picks up a large object, such as a table, to throw on the other's head, as if suddenly disgusted by his forbidden love.

Finally, the weaker of the two submits to his dominant partner, just as they have known would happen from those first moments when they met and sized up one another's spray-on tans. The winner is awarded an enormous sparkly belt, not unlike those worn by broad-shouldered, cat-fighting actresses in 1980s nighttime dramas.

Foe or Faux?

Test your knowledge of vituperation by determining if the following is an insult or not.

I was truly shocked to hear that you spent all yesterday afternoon engaged in runcation, Arnie.

This is not an insult. Arnie was weeding his garden.

Eric has remarked to me more than once that he finds this event a thrilling, testosterone-charged evening of machismo, which I believe goes a long way toward explaining why he does not have a girlfriend.

In reality, most men do not look good in stretch fabrics, and throwing tables on people's heads is likely to get you arrested. As for you, dear reader, even if you do not feel the need to overstate your masculinity by grappling erotically with hulking coworkers in your cubicle, you may occasionally be called upon to prove yourself in verbal sparring and in this arena, I would like to help. To paraphrase a great speaker, the ultimate measure of a man is not where he stands in a gold lamé onesie, but where he stands in a pair of chinos.

Get that Hoopty Outta My Parking Spot! How to Address Usurpers at the Club

Dear Lady Snark,

I was at the country club yesterday when I noticed a car in the lot parked across two spaces, one of which belongs to my wife. I don't mean it was parked diagonally across two spots—the car was so gigantic that it required two spaces. It looked like a tank, actually. The owner was nowhere in sight, so I asked the front desk and was told that it belonged to a "Redonkulus Killah." I wasn't able to find him and the tow truck couldn't bear the weight of the car to pull it out of the spot, so my wife had to park in the visitor's lot. How can I give this Mr. Killah a piece of my mind when I do see him?

Morton

Boca Raton, Florida

My Dear,

I am not sure I would offer Mr. Killah a piece of your mind, on the off chance that he might take you literally. I met the gentleman in question at a charity auction a few years ago and the proportions of his vehicle, as you describe them, are not dissimilar from the proportions of his person relative to ordinary beings.

My understanding from my friend Countess Horswick, who introduced him to me, is that he is a "gangsta rapper." Further enquiries to Eric and Amelia confirm this. Amelia also assured me that while he is not an actual gangster, he owns a number of semi-automatic weapons and engages in the drug trade. This distinction was a bit unclear to me, but I believe the principal differences between Mr. Killah and Al Capone are that Mr. Killah makes a secondary income from a kind of speak-singing (like Rex Harrison in *My Fair Lady*, but with more drums) and does not wear a hat.

Mr. Killah was quite engaging and entertained us with tales of his hardscrabble youth, a modern-day Horatio Alger story in which the plucky hero exponentially increases his take-home pay by selling angel dust instead of newspapers or matches.

About a month later, I met some of his business associates, who had just finished a game of golf at a country club in Connecticut. I do not remember all of their names, though two were brothers whose surname was Dawg.

One of them (I believe his name was Mr. Kripp) told me that although he enjoyed the amenities at the club and had found the tennis pro to have a great deal of useful advice regarding his backhand, he was dissatisfied with his parking space for the very reason you describe.

While I engaged in a rather lengthy discussion with him on this point, I was struck with his speaking style, which was quite colorful. In fact, I was so enamored of this unusual lexicon that I took notes, some of which I will share with you. As Mr. Killah uses the same expressions, I believe you might find a small primer on this "rap" language useful in your dealings with him.

First of all, when encountering such a problem, you should not make the error of simply pointing out the largeness of the interloper's sports utility vehicle, as shown in the example below.

> Sir, I wonder if you could use a more reasonably sized conveyance to attend the tournament tomorrow. You might experience difficulty opening the doors in such a behemoth.

Your transgressor is well aware that his car is large. That is why he bought it.

Nor should you assume that such a person will be unfamiliar with the word *behemoth* and therefore miss your slur. As I learned from Mr. Kripp, those who "spit rhymes" for a living must live and die by the thesaurus.

Again, I would advise against it for your personal safety, but if you feel that the provocation was such that you must throw down the gauntlet, try addressing Mr. Killah in his preferred parlance when shouting from your car window. This will give you the element of surprise as you "drive by."

> **Yo, mayn! Get that hoopty outta my spot or get mercked.**
> **Translation:** I beg your pardon, sir. I must ask you to move your inferior automobile unless you wish for me to assassinate you.

Of course, you mean you will assassinate his character with the club president, but he doesn't need to know that. And don't worry about your car being scratched when he pulls in and opens his door after you. That lime green "candy" paint and the crystal studded spinners cost more than a semester's tuition at Miss Grandy's Country Day School, so he will not risk a blemish on his own vehicle. Here are a few more useful phrases you might use to insult Mr. Killah, if intimidation does not work:

Stop frontin'. You ain't all that.

Translation: You may pretend to be an upstanding member of society by carrying a bag of designer clubs, but like the ostensibly oak surface of your custom-made dashboard, it is only a thin veneer, easily revealed to anyone with breeding and a utility knife.

Shit, homey—you get that bucket from the popo for droppin' a dime?

Translation: I find your taste in automobiles shocking, my friend! Your jalopy is of such questionable provenance that I am inclined to think the police pawned some impounded wreck off on you as payment for informing on your former associates in illicit trade.

You ain't hood no more.

Translation: Although your insistence on spending time in the company of genteel persons has not made a silk purse from a sow's ear, the proximity to refinement has removed your "street credibility." Unfortunately, this puts you in danger from those who still "keep it real" in much the same way that a baby bird held by a child and imbued with human scent will be not only abandoned by its mother, but also pecked to death and eaten by its siblings.

Foe or Faux?

Test your knowledge of vituperation by determining if the following is an insult or not.

Watch out! After a few beers, Seth here gets pretty lachrymose.

This is an insult. Drinking makes Seth cry.

Happily, Mr. Kripp did not "spray" Mr. Peterson (who was assigned the spot next to his) with bullets to expand his parking options, as was his original plan. I mentioned that it had been my experience that regardless of whether one is arrested by the "Five-O," the mere whiff of scandal is enough to put one's membership in jeopardy. Ultimately, he merely drove slowly past that gentleman's home displaying his AK-

47 for a number of subsequent evenings until Mr. Peterson informed the club president that he would be more than happy to share.

Incidentally, you should have no trouble identifying Mr. Killah when you see him, as he wears a name tag. But don't worry—you won't mistake him for the help because his "Killah" label, which hangs on a "dookey rope" around his neck, is made from a pound and a half of gold and studded with jewels to match his teeth. I wish you the best of luck!

Cordially,

Lady Arabella Snark

Malediction 101: How to Avoid a Bar Fight

Perhaps you are troubled by the behavior of a lout at the local watering hole, but you just don't have the courage to knock a chip off his shoulder. No worries. Use these little-known insults and you may return to your frozen daiquiri unharmed.

> **Perhaps if you didn't drink so many beers, you would be a bit less enormously *pyriform*.**
> pyriform: shaped like a pear

Did I hear you say you were leaving early to take home some milk? I must say, that gives your behavior a most *uxorious* appearance.

uxorious: too devoted to one's wife

Sir, your remarks do not inspire terror in my soul, as I have observed your *poltroonery* on several occasions in the past.

poltroonery: cowardice

I'm afraid there is something about the way your little finger points away from your longneck that makes you look a bit *effete*.

effete: delicate and effeminate

I notice your usual companions are on the other side of the bar. Do you suppose it's because you're so *feculent* this evening?

feculent: covered with feces

Ring-A-Ding-A-Sing Sing

Dear Lady Snark,

Sorry I missed you at the Brevard's house party last weekend. I couldn't come out East because, apparently, someone had noticed the millions of dollars I'd siphoned off those retirement funds. My lawyer says they're going to try to put me into a real prison instead of the tennis camp kind because they couldn't find my assistant and there was a little blood in his abandoned car. I know you've been to prison, so I wondered if you could offer me some pointers on sounding tough and intimidating.

Terrance

Brentwood, California

My Dear,

I'm not sure "tough and intimidating" is the way to go for a man whose idea of roughing it is to forgo his weekly facial. However, if you are smart, you will use your legal know-how, pharmaceutical connections, and large sums of money to "click up" (join a gang) advantageously.

Once you have established yourself as a vital member of your group, you will be in a better position to taunt newcomers with the "tough and intimidating" lingo of your new "set." Here are a few examples I recall from my days in "the joint."

Yo, fish! You mess with us and you'll be eatin' joot balls in the cooler.

Translation: Worthless new prisoner, my compatriots and I are the powerful ones in this penitentiary. If you cross us, you will find yourself in solitary confinement eating nasty leftovers.

You'd best dummy up about this caviar and Sean Don or we'll invite you to a blanket party.

Translation: You would do well to refrain from telling the guards about our luxurious but illegal picnic; if you do not, we will wrap you in a blanket and beat you senseless.

You ain't my road dog. Back off or meet my banger.

Translation: You and I are not good friends, so please leave me alone. Otherwise, I will be compelled to attack you with my homemade knife.

Foe or Faux?

Test your knowledge of vituperation by determining if the following is an insult or not.

So, Ned, I heard you and Zeke were out weequashing last night. Good thing the police didn't catch you two!

This is not an insult. Ned and Zeke were spearfishing (which is illegal in most states) by torchlight.

Be sure to have your "homies" with you for protection when you voice these sentiments. And I do hope you enjoy your stay there. I myself had some of the most pleasant times of my life while incarcerated. It was just like boarding school, except with better uniforms and more drugs.

Cordially,

Lady Arabella Snark

Nice Shot, Girly-Man! Asserting Your Masculinity in Sporting Events

Dear Lady Snark,

I was recently transferred from our company's London office to a new business centre in the American Midwest. As a man who takes pride in custom-made suits and has an intimate acquaintance with Europe's top wine bars, I am finding the culture shock overwhelming.

But that isn't my real predicament. I believe one of my new coworkers has developed a bit of a tendre for me. I had never played softball before (I'm more of a squash and cricket man) and found myself rather inept at the game when we played it last week at the company picnic. Mitch, a large, rather beefy fellow from our R&D team, kept calling out "candy ass!" and "You go, sweetie!" when I stepped up to the plate. His sexually suggestive remarks made me uncomfortable. How can I tell him I am not interested?

Neville

Stoat City, Iowa

Foe or Faux?

Test your knowledge of vituperation by determining if the following is an insult or not.

Arnie, I always assumed your demeanor was reflective of the orchidectomy you had when you got married.

This is an insult. An orchidectomy is the surgical removal of the testes.

My Dear,

I don't think that will be necessary. Based on his remarks, I think it is fair to assume that Mitch does not like you in that way, or in any way. As you have already discovered, there are a number of things that don't translate across the pond and based on my recollection of the Midwest, I believe this difference could best be summed up by a comparison of your stated interests: Where you now live, wine comes in a box, cricket is an insect, and squash is something you do to crickets.

Likewise, "candy ass" is not intended as a compliment to your derrière, but rather as a suggestion that you are less than macho. Mitch's comments are intended to voice his disapprobation of your dress, behavior, and softball skills (not to mention your accent), all of which scream "God Save the Queen!" to his bulky ears. To men like Mitch, manliness is paramount; to Mitch in particular, you are about as manly as the sheep he lost his virginity to in 1985.

To regain your reputation will be a two-step process: First, you must rebuild your image as a studly he-man; then you must teach Mitch not to slight you.

Begin by paying attention to your public persona: Do not mention your devotion to light operas by Gilbert and Sullivan; do not bemoan the lack of fine haberdasheries in the area; do not use the word *haberdashery* in conversation; do not offer anyone the fantastic recipe you used for trifle at your last garden party; do not have garden parties; do not eat trifle.

Having learned to restrain your natural impulses, you should then try to adopt local habits and mannerisms that will signify your virility. For example, you might learn to play horseshoes, belch publicly, or feign an interest in corn hybridization.

Once you have overcome the obstacle of your own sophistication, you will be ready to defend yourself as a man by trading barbs with Mitch.

"But surely, I have no argument with Mitch!" you might say, "Let bygones be bygones. I have already forgotten his remarks regarding the delectability of my nether regions." However, in order to maintain your image as a "real man," you will need to challenge anyone who has brought your status into question.

Wee Willie Winkie

Men like Mitch take pride in their hulking immensity, so it is quite easy to disturb their equanimity by suggesting that they are, in fact, petite. If Mitch is sufficiently insecure, the fact that you are half his size will do little or nothing to soften the accusation.

What you say must be both rude and direct, as subtlety may result in unintended compliments. Here's an example from Barclay, an acquaintance of mine who is occasionally required to visit Indiana for business. During these forays, he is usually obliged to play golf with Sid, the plant manager. Barclay does not like Sid because he feels uncomfortable around men whose necks and waists are the same size. To cut Sid down to a more diminutive size, he makes this misguided and fruitless attempt.

Barclay: Sid, you're looking very slim. Have you lost weight?

> **Sid:** Thanks, buddy! Yeah, that old push mower takes off a few pounds.

A far better effect can be achieved with more specific and direct comparisons.

> **Barclay:** You're quite the pencil-neck runt, Sid. I do hope that nine iron isn't too heavy for you.

The average pencil is less than an inch in circumference, exponentially smaller than Sid's neck. Coupled with runt (the smallest of the offspring born to a farm animal) this phrase could make Sid feel as though he's been robbed of his reproductive organs.

> **Sid:** How dare you! Now I'm going to sink to the grass in emotional distress and cry like a little girl.

Of course, the ideal response on Sid's part has been supplied. It is also possible that Sid will crush Barclay's skull with his nine iron. If you think it might be safer, you could try cloaking such a remark in ostensible flattery. Here are some examples, again from the game of golf.

Whoa, Nelly! What a drive, Half-Pint.
Translation: I cannot hide my astonishment that a tiny little girl like you managed to propel the golf ball almost all the way to Mr. Oleson's store.

I think your grip is really improving, Pee-Wee.
Translation: Wow! Your teeny little hands are almost big enough to encircle your club.

You go, Bitsy—what a slice!
Translation: I admire your ability to hit the great big ball into the faraway hole despite being so Lilliputian.

Barclay could also intimate, directly or indirectly, that his male opponent is somehow handicapped by his feminine side.

Nice shot, girly-man!
Translation: Your golf is nearly as impressive as your French manicure.

Once you've mastered this art, it will only take a few belittling words to make Mitch cry into his knockoff-brand shampoo in the shower room. On the other hand, "talking trash" to fend off unwanted suggestions that you are a "nancy" may potentially result in physical altercations, so it would be wise to invest in some martial arts lessons as a precaution. Take care and I do hope that, over time, you will learn to enjoy tractor pulls and eating corn with your hands.

Cordially,

Lady Arabella Snark

Foe or Faux?

Test your knowledge of vituperation by determining if the following is an insult or not.

So, Red, I understand your wife has become a thespian. Doesn't that bother you?

This is not an insult. Red's wife has taken up acting.

The Quixotic 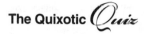 Quiz

Test Your Knowledge of Gangsta Rap

In the following quotes from Redonkulus Killah's well-received 2007 album, *Popo Platter,* is he threatening to kill someone, trying to seduce someone, or something else entirely? Choose the closest translation.

1. Oh, you think you so cute, lil' mama, But tonight I'm bringin' you my llama.

   A. You believe you are attractive, Mom. And it's true! That's why I'm going to give you my Peruvian pet. Happy Mother's Day!

   B. You have a high opinion of yourself, lady, which is why I'm bringing a gun to shoot you tonight.

   C. You think you are attractive, girlfriend, and you are. That's why I'm going to give you a luxury car this evening.

2. Oh, you're so thicky thick, I wanna hit you with my magic stick.

   A. You are extremely plump, which I find desirable. If you enjoy sadomasochistic games, perhaps we could arrange for a meeting later on.

   B. You have an exceptionally nice figure, so I'd like to have sex with you.

   C. You are so incredibly stupid that it makes me want to shoot you.

3. I'm gon' ice you out till you're frozen.

   A. My plan is to lock you into a butcher's storage unit until you die of hypothermia.

continued

B.   I'm going to shoot you until I have entirely exhausted my supply of ammunition so that I can be sure you are dead.

C.   I am going to buy you a large collection of diamond jewelry.

4.   Chris said we could meet up in the trap, Yeah tonight I'm gonna peel a cap.

A.   Chris invited me to meet him for an illegal drug deal; what he doesn't realize is that I plan to shoot him in the head.

B.   I'm meeting Chris at her apartment for a fun-filled evening of unsafe sex.

C.   Chris and I are going to meet at the local bar to drink some beers.

5.   Fee-Fee—Fi-Fi—Fo-Fo—Fum-Fum, Let's play some games like red-rum, red-rum.

A.   I really enjoy children's stories and plan to incorporate "Jack and the Beanstalk" into a game for my daughter's birthday party.

B.   Let's play a game that involves drinking rum and cranberry juice every time a television character uses a word that contains any of the sounds above.

C.   Let's go kill somebody.

6.   Shawty, if you pop-pop-pop it, I'll give you some cabbage.

A.   Sir, I'd like to hire you for an assassination.

B.   Girl, if you dance erotically, I'll give you some money.

C.   Friend, if you wouldn't mind opening this beer for me, I'll let you have some of my coleslaw.

Answer key: 1. B; 2. B; 3. C; 4. A; 5. C; 6. B

nine. I Don't Like Mondays, Tuesdays, Wednesdays, Thursdays, or Fridays

In which we consider the benefits and disadvantages of WORK, & discover that the difficulties of actually getting a job are exceeded only by the PUTRESCENCE of having one, despite the opportunities to attack your boss with an EPONYMOUS INSULT, confuse TROGLODYTIC COLLEAGUES with ARCANE HOSTILITIES, or write ostensibly kind (but actually brutal) letters filled with FAINT PRAISE for former subordinates you wish had fallen into an ABYSS.

How to Get a Rent Free Apartment Without Really Trying

I dislike Herman Melville and have never managed to make it past page twenty of that tedious whale story of his. However, due to circumstances beyond my control, I have read his short story "Bartleby the Scrivener" and would like to take this opportunity to share its insights on office life with you now.

A few weeks after Babe Paley's funeral (which I thought it would be in poor taste to attend under the circumstances but went to anyway) I was on my way down to the Vineyard when I found myself stuck in traffic. As I had nothing to do, I asked my chauffeur, Jean Henri, for the emergency gin flask in the glove compartment and began to read aloud from the dog-eared book of dull nineteenth-century New England authors I'd stolen from a bed and breakfast in Marblehead.

Melville's tale recounts the non-adventures of Bartleby, who first (understandably) refuses to work as a human photocopier and then inexplicably refuses to leave his workplace, continuing to live there even after being fired. When asked to complete office tasks or go home, he tells his employer, "I would prefer not to." Not surprisingly, his coworkers find this creepy, and eventually his entire office is forced to change locations to get away from him.

I saw this story as a cautionary tale for human resources professionals, but Jean Henri observed that living in your office would really save you a lot of money, especially if your salary was as low as Bartleby's.

Foe or Faux?

Test your knowledge of vituperation by determining if the following is an insult or not.

What an unusual presentation, Sue! I wouldn't be surprised if your job becomes filipendulous after that!

This is an insult. Sue's job will be hanging by a thread.

This notion of salaries and money-saving was something of a revelation to me; I'd always assumed people took office jobs to avoid spending time with their families. Even so, shacking up with thirty other unhappy souls in a badly lit taupe maze that reeks of carpet cleaner could easily be worse than shacking up with four in a suburban ranch house.

If I had to work for a living, I think I would prefer a more solitary career, such as being a hit man. Assassins, after all, are never tormented

195

with a hundred nearly identical pictures of Sue's baby being licked on the mouth by a worm-ridden puppy, nor must they suffer the noxious "silent but deadly" farts of Jim in the next cubicle.

On the other hand, assassins can only kill each target once. As a cubicle worker, you have a daily opportunity to debase and humiliate people who cannot escape you. In this light, I suppose, apart from the smell, the long hours, the degradation, and the unsavory company, work isn't all bad.

Demoralizing a colleague until he can't take it anymore and hacks off his own head with the paper cutter will give you more of a sense of accomplishment than a rifle shot ever could; it is also much less likely to put you in prison. Just for fun, see how many insults in this chapter it takes before your colleagues begin to decapitate themselves using office supplies.

Malediction 101: How to Fire Someone

Terminating a despised employee should always be backed up with a good reason if you want to avoid legal action. Ensure that your company is off the hook by giving one of these.

Gosh, Brad, we're sorry to let you go, but I'm afraid that the *haruspicy* you've been employing to create business projections has led to a rash of complaints about the cleanliness of the break room.

haruspicy: examining ritually killed animals' intestines to tell the future

Amber, it's great that you like to keep the old traditions alive, but there are more modern methods than *dactylonomy* in accounting.

dactylonomy: counting on your fingers

As much as you believe our CEO is an *energumen*, Celeste, you can't just follow him into the elevator and throw holy water on him every morning.

energumen: someone possessed by a demon

Janice, while the company has no specific policy on *polyandry*, the fact that your situation involves three gentlemen from our direct competition gives us no choice but to let you go.

polyandry: marriage of one woman to several men

I'm sure your being so *ventripotent* is useful in county fair competitions, George, but it's driving our bakery into the ground, so we're replacing you.

ventripotent: the ability and desire to eat a lot

Troglodytes in the Copy Room

Dear Lady Snark,

Last week, my manager couldn't find anyone to copy a report for him to distribute at the weekly meeting (because we were all in the conference room waiting for him). Based on the physical evidence, he apparently jammed our copier, went to a different machine on the floor below, and while waiting for that machine to finish the job, tossed a toner cartridge from hand to hand until it hit the floor and exploded, leaving black dust on every surface of the room. Then he came to the meeting covered with soot and slapped everyone on the back so we had to walk around the building with hand prints on our shoulders. (Actually, Jenny had to go meet clients afterward with what looked like an obscene tattoo on the rear of her skirt.) I say my boss is an idiot, but my office mate Arlene thinks he is an imbecile. What would you call him?

Puneet
Bend, Oregon

My Dear,

With the limited information you have given me, I would have to agree with Arlene. According to Henry Goddard, the eugenicist of questionable ethics who created that hierarchy, imbeciles are smarter than idiots and less intelligent than morons. In fact, idiots have an IQ of 25 or less (100 being average for "normal" people) so it seems unlikely that your boss fits into that category. If he did, it probably would not have occurred to him to try to destroy a second machine. He would still be standing in your copy room staring blankly at the paper jam symbol, mouth agape.

However, I wouldn't call him either if I wanted to keep my job (and presumably you do, or you wouldn't still be there). That doesn't mean you have to be nice, though. Given his level of intelligence, you can probably get away with insulting him to his face by using words he doesn't know. This works especially well if you take the effort emphasize a few positive words, as shown:

What you say: Your *hardworking* sudiferous glands must make you terribly *appealing* to others who share your pinguitude!

What you mean: You sweat like a pig and are thus likely to attract others who, like you, resemble them in heft.

If you are lucky, he will only hear "hardworking" and "appealing." Here are a couple more examples to help you get started:

What you say: It's really a *great reflection* on the company that they hire cretinous loobies like you.

What you mean: Hiring mentally and physically stunted clods like you demonstrates the company's dedication to helping the less fortunate.

What you say: Wow, you've been *so busy* aestivating for the last three months! You are the *king* of torpor!!

What you mean: You basically slept through an entire summer of work. It's almost like you're unconscious.

Aestivating, I should add, is the opposite of hibernating. Animals that typically sleep through the hot season include frogs, lizards, and snakes, so your boss is in good company.

Cordially,

Lady Arabella Snark

Dear Lady Snark,

I was recently promoted and am now supervising a group of total slackers. They seem to be under the impression that they can just leave whenever they feel like it and are usually out the door by eight o'clock at night, even though there is still work to do. What's worse is that none of them seems to remember my name. They all call me Mr. Legree instead of Mr. Green (my real name). What is wrong with these people?

Alphonse

Kermit, West Virginia

My Dear,

I would say that their biggest problem is that they are working for you. And I am sure that they can remember your name; they just chose to christen you with an eponymous insult that draws a parallel between your management philosophy and that of Simon Legree, a cruel slave owner in the novel *Uncle Tom's Cabin*.

As you are probably aware, eponyms are names that are based on the names of actual or imaginary people. As in your case, this can be a negative association. Thomas Crapper, for example, may or may not have been the inventor of the flush toilet, but the finer points of that etymology are of little comfort to the plumber's heirs as they enter junior high school.

In case your subordinates tire of this insult, I've included a short list of other eponyms you might hear from them in the quiz below. See how many you can match to their deeper meanings!

Cordially,

Lady Arabella Snark

Foe or Faux?

Test your knowledge of vituperation by determining if the following is an insult or not.

So, Zack, your job at the zoo must be quite different since now everyone thinks you were responsible for the defalcation!

This is an insult. Zack is guilty of embezzling.

Quiz

The Eponymous Slight or, Your Supervisor Is a Crappy Bozo

. . . .

1.	Captain Bligh!	A.	Listen, you clown, why don't you take your joke of a report and use it to scoop up some elephant crap.
2.	Dunce!	B.	Uncultured boor! If there were a tree in the building, you'd climb it to poop on what's left of the arts funding you just cut.
3.	Bozo!	C.	News flash, you prehistoric moron: They may be immune to viruses, but no one has used an abacus for creating spreadsheets since you started working here in 1842.
4.	Luddite!	D.	Get with the program, you pointy-headed idiot!
5.	Yahoo!	E.	One more demand for overtime and we're taking off for Tahiti and leaving you to finish the project yourself, asshole!

Answer Key:

1.   Captain Bligh!: E

This reportedly cruel British naval officer's problems in maintaining employee satisfaction have long been an object lesson for managers. After being brutally lashed and told that their benefits package (in the form of exotic island

continued

203

beauties) was going to be sharply cut, Bligh's crew took over the ship and went on vacation, leaving their captain to drift in a leaky rowboat between cannibal islands. The moral of this story? You should never whip people unless they are paying you handsomely to do it.

2.   Dunce!: D

The most interesting thing about medieval scholar John Scotus Duns is that his students reportedly stabbed him to death with pens. The second most interesting is that he thought you could get smarter by wearing pointy hats. Long after his death, Duns's followers rejected new ways of thinking only to discover that all you get from wearing pointy hats is a pointy head.

3.   Bozo!: A

The laughter! The pranks! The hiding in terror under your seat to get away from the pointy-haired clown. Kind of like your job, except now you hide under the desk. Note that bozos have pointy hair, while dunces have pointy heads (though the two are often found together).

4.   Luddite!: C

The Luddites of yesteryear, under the leadership of the (possibly fictitious) Ned Ludd, despised technology and hacked "newfangled" factory machinery to pieces because it was taking away their jobs. If your boss screams at the computer as if it were a sentient being, he may qualify as a modern equivalent, even if he is too out-of-shape to follow up by throwing it out the window.

5.   Yahoo!: B

In Gulliver's Travels, the Yahoos were a group of dirty animals that lacked "teachableness, civility and cleanliness" and enjoyed throwing their own feces on people from trees. Unlike the uncultured brutes in Swift's story, today's Yahoos are rewarded for their coarse stupidity by being given the right to fire you.

Secretary of the Damned with Faint Praise

Dear Lady Snark,

I've just received an e-mail asking for a recommendation for a terrible former employee. Why do incompetent people I fired give me as a reference? Don't they know I can't say anything good?

Jason

Oshkosh, Wisconsin

My Dear,

They list you because they know you can't say anything bad. Sometimes, I long for the frank assessments of yesteryear when you could wistfully remark, "Indeed, we will all miss Fred and the embezzled money we are pretty sure he transferred to a secret account in the Cayman Islands." But times have changed, and the threat of being sued means you must resort to subterfuge to undermine the future careers of bad employees.

Foe or Faux?

Test your knowledge of vituperation by determining if the following is an insult or not.

So, Zack, your job at the zoo must be quite different since now everyone thinks you were responsible for the defalcation!

This is an insult. Zack is guilty of embezzling.

It's a pity, but it is possible to get around the problem by damning the former thorn in your side with faint praise. Should you be called on the phone for such an assessment, be sure to say positive things, but use a tone of voice that belies their meaning, as if you were remembering a particularly vile strain of syphilis you picked up at a bordello in the Crimean War and just couldn't shake, no matter how much penicillin you took.

If the recommendation is in writing, remember that since references are generally couched in the most hyperbolically laudatory terms, words like *competent* and *acceptable* read like burning coals of condemnation. If you word your letter carefully, human resources will read between the lines and see that your stated meaning and your actual meaning are worlds apart, as shown below.

To Whom It May Concern:

Jessica M. was a "unique" employee. [She was frighteningly strange.] She was always remarkably relaxed, even when she was standing too close to the dangerous heavy machinery in the plant. [We're pretty sure she was on drugs, but it's possible that she just has the IQ of a squirrel.] She was very modest about her nearly adequate skills in operating computer equipment. [She spent three weeks pressing the computer keyboard's "home" button, thinking it would transport her back to her apartment for lunch.] However, even though it was not part of her job, she had excellent phone skills, which she used incessantly to increase her vision of the future. [She made a lot of toll calls to her Philippine psychic.] During her two-week tenure, she left a mark on several employees, ensuring that they will never forget her. [Three valuable workers were nearly blinded in accidents involving her press-on nail extensions.]

I wish you the best of luck. [Run!]

I would also wish you the best of luck, Jason, but I suspect that yours would improve if you would just start making reference calls about potential employees at your own company.

Cordially,

Lady Arabella Snark

On the Social Advantages of Losing Your Job Shortly after Thanksgiving

Dear Lady Snark,

Friday, my office is supposed to have a party for a couple of hours at a local "bistro" to celebrate the fact that, now that our latest product has shipped, we will only have to work seventy hours a week instead of ninety. I don't suppose I can spend more than half of it hiding in the bathroom without arousing suspicion that I'm not a "team player."

However, most of my coworkers are pretty irritating, even in small doses. I am especially worried that one of the sales reps, Kendra Blanket, is going to send me over the edge. Based on my last few conversations with her, she is going to complain in a fake way about how it's so difficult to get married (she's engaged and I'm not) because you have to spend so much time being fitted for the dress and deciding where to go on your honeymoon. She doesn't mean it. I think she's just saying that to make me jealous. May I kill her?

Elspeth

Truth or Consequences, New Mexico

Foe or Faux?

Test your knowledge of vituperation by determining if the following is an insult or not.

Jake, your behavior around the new manager brings to mind a cephalopod.

This is an insult. Cephalopods are marine mollusks like octopuses; Jake is a suck-up.

My Dear,

Of course she is doing it to make you jealous. But you need to recognize that she is setting herself up. To feign insecurity when you actually feel superior is the verbal equivalent of walking into a cage of Komodo dragons with a ham tied around your neck. (By the way, the authorities still haven't determined how that very thing happened to my second husband, Michel, the inveterate gambler and womanizer.)

Kendra is counting on you to appreciate her false modesty and correct it, like this:

Oh, Kendra, how can you say that? It must be *so great* to get married! If only I, too, could be *so lucky*.

That's more trust than you should have in anyone who isn't named favorably in your will. When you talk to Kendra, all you have to do to is nod your head and concur with her negative assessment. It *is* terrible that she's getting married. *Thank God* it's not you. It must be *so difficult* to refit the dress every few weeks as she gains more weight. And so on. How could you be more "polite"?

{

Foe or Faux?

Test your knowledge of vituperation by determining if the following is an insult or not.

Mark, I'm afraid the antipodal nature of your office has been causing communication problems.

This is not an insult. Mark's office is on the other side of the earth.

The Vainer They Come, the Harder They Bawl

If you need more examples, here are some from a master of this technique: Bethany Mathis, of the firm Pill and Birch. Here, she and her coworkers are enjoying watered-down drinks and scanty snacks at a holiday office party hosted by her boss, Millicent Pill.

Everyone knows that Norman, who started a year after Bethany did, has just been given a bonus equal to Bethany's annual salary for making a major sale to his uncle's company. However, Norman is inept in the game of one-upsmanship. He decides to rub her nose in it by complaining about his imaginary financial woes.

> **Norman:** My god, the mortgage on my third tropical island vacation home is killing me.
>
> **Bethany:** If you need to save money, have you considered cutting back on your cocaine habit? Oh, hi Millicent. Great cheese ball!

As you can see, when attacked by a larger opponent, Bethany does not resist, but simply allows him to injure himself with the weight and force of his own stupidity. Occasionally, such large-headed persons will set themselves up to fall so beautifully that the slightest touch will knock them over, as shown by this exchange with Pablo, the assistant manager.

> **Pablo:** It's difficult being on top at this company. Everyone hates to be around a winner.
>
> **Bethany:** Oh, do you think that's the reason you're such a pariah at the office? I'd always figured it was your B.O.

In another corner, Bethany's brawny officemate Rick kicks metaphorical sand into the eyes of her scrawny friend Jerome as she looks on in disdain.

> **Rick:** Do you know how difficult it is to buy a suit once you've really bulked up? Unless I get one custom-made, the neck is so small that it totally cuts off my circulation.
>
> **Bethany:** Gosh, that's terrible that not enough blood can get to your brain, Rick. I'd noticed your intelligence had decreased since you started going to the gym so much, but I'd assumed it was the steroids.

Finally, a true master can use the advanced form of neither agreeing nor disagreeing. Here, Kyle, the self-styled office "ladies' man," boasts to Bethany of his latest conquest—perhaps fantasizing that his luck with the ladies will make him irresistible to her as well. As Bethany knows, when you are unlikely to be fact checked you may parry such idiocy with a direct lie.

> **Kyle:** God, it's a curse to be so attractive to women. I came here with Jennifer, the office sexpot, but Chris, that hoochie temp from sales, was making eyes at me, so I told Jennifer to take a hike. And the best part is that Chris is leaving for San Francisco tomorrow, so no strings, baby!
>
> **Bethany:** Chris is a man.

And yes, if none of these work for you, violence is always an option, though I recommend a different venue than the party itself if you don't wish to be caught. Still, if you can't resist, once you've taught the other girls to do your laundry properly, prison is not as bad as you might think.

Cordially,

Lady Arabella Snark

The Quixotic *Quiz*

Test Your Knowledge of Excruciatingly Awful Coworkers

There are so many ways to say, "I hate you." Though space constraints prevent a complete listing, here are a few nicknames for those colleagues who make your work life a bonfire of hell, minus the s'mores and sing-a-longs. Match each clue on the left to the coworker it describes on the right.

Clue		**Coworker**	
1.	footwear enthusiast	A.	pinhead
2.	theatrical ruler	B.	slimeball
3.	German for decoration	C.	slacker

Clue		Coworker	
4.	sideshow performer with miniscule mind	D.	bootlicker
5.	opposite of tighter	E.	fool
6.	devious member of Mustelidae family	F.	drama queen
7.	revolting Christmas dessert	G.	ass
8.	like Feste in *Twelfth Night*	H.	fruitcake
9.	slippery sphere	I.	weasel
10.	what you sit on, which is not a chair	J.	schmuck

Answer Key: 1. D; 2. F; 3. J; 4. A; 5. C; 6. I; 7. H; 8. E; 9. B; 10. G

Legal Disclaimer

In which we discover, to our complete astonishment, that many of the RECOMMENDATIONS made by Lady Snark are DANGEROUS & some even ILLEGAL in many locales, &, moreover, that she has no intention of paying our BAIL, visiting us in PRISON, or covering our medical expenses should we aggravate someone to the point that they BREAK OUR LEGS or leave us HIDEOUSLY DISFIGURED.

Terms and Conditions of Use

By purchasing this book, you (hereinafter "the reader," except for those portions of the contract where it just seemed too bothersome to write in the third person) hereby acknowledge that you have read and agree to the terms and conditions that are set out in this contract, regardless of whether the font is too small for you to actually see them. This agreement also applies to any person who comes into permanent or temporary possession of the book or any of its contents in any manner, including but not limited to receiving it as a gift, checking it out of the library, reading over someone's shoulder on the subway, hearing portions recited aloud over the phone, or finding it wedged under the mattress between the "adult" magazines while staying at a friend's house.

1. Assumption of Risk

The reader acknowledges that many of the activities described in this book, such as using what might be perceived as aggressive verbiage in bars, handling poisonous reptiles, and publicly criticizing a manager's moronic business plan, are inherently dangerous and are likely to result in something unfortunate happening to you. That is the reader's problem, not the problem of Arabella Bainbridge St. Germaine Wang Montague Fishtweed, Right Honourable Countess of Snark (hereinafter "Lady Snark"), as will be outlined in more detail below. Nor does Lady Snark have any obligation to provide the reader with bandages or ice if he or she gets paper cuts turning the pages of this book or hurts his or her foot by dropping the book thereon, respectively. Should be you become so engrossed in this book that you are struck by a sixteen-wheel truck as you read it while walking across the street, Lady Snark will be flattered, but will not visit you in the hospital

2. Disclaimer of Reliability

With respect to the contents of this book, Lady Snark assumes absolutely zero legal liability or responsibility for the accuracy, completeness, or usefulness of this information and advice. It is important to remember that Lady Snark was well acquainted with various counterculture figures as a young woman; certain substances she experimented with in the late sixties may have impaired her ability to recall every detail of her life in lucid detail. This is something her stepchildren frequently bring up when she embarrasses them with what they claim are inaccurate stories about their childhoods in front of potential life partners. Therefore, the contents of this book are presented "as is," which, if it helps you to better comprehend the implications, is the same terminology department stores use for a delicate size-six chiffon blouse on the sale rack that has been tried on by hundreds of hopeful but doomed size-twelve persons.

3. Disclaimer of Liability

As concerns this book, Lady Snark makes no warranty, express or implied, including the warranties of merchantability and/or fitness for a particular purpose. In no event will Lady Snark be liable for any direct, incidental, special, or consequential damages or any loss of life or revenue or anything else bad that happens as a result of the reader's availing themselves of the materials contained in this book. "Bad things" include, but are not limited to:

i. Loss of income or inheritance. Any loss of income or inheritance, including salaries, bonuses, homes, automobiles, money, boats, gold coins, jewelry, works of art such as paintings or sculptures, et cetera, as a result of the reader's own stupidity in using the contents of this book are solely the reader's responsibility. The reader also acknowledges that sharing information with Lady Snark regarding a wealthy older relative could lead to Lady Snark becoming the beneficiary of said inheritance instead of the reader. In the event of such a relative's sudden demise (shortly after their marriage to Lady Snark) from any method(s), including but not limited to poisoning, drowning, a mysterious heart attack, being crushed by an elephant, or contracting a rare and fatal form of dysentery previously believed to be carried only by the extinct spectacled cormorant, the reader agrees not to challenge Lady Snark in any way regarding her portion of the inheritance.

ii. Imprisonment. The reader acknowledges that any seemingly criminal advice contained in this book is presented "just for fun" and the active use of this information is strictly prohibited under this Agreement. Acting upon any of the aforementioned "just for fun" suggestions is likely to result in the reader's incarceration; Lady Snark has no legal responsibility for the reader's actions, attorney's fees, or bail money. On the other hand, should you make any profits from criminal activity inspired by this book, you agree to share these profits with Lady Snark.

iii. Accidental death or dismemberment. Much of the advice contained in this book could lead to the reader's accidental or, more likely, intentional death at the hands of someone who is unhappy with the reader's behavior and it is therefore the reader's sole responsibility to avoid this. For dismemberment, see Clause 6, Severability, below.

iv. Dissolution of marriage. Some people are extremely sensitive; this may include the reader's spouse. You and you alone are responsible for determining whether your beloved will be willing to be referred to as fat, ugly, or stupid and accept all consequences of such remarks to be your own problem, including but not limited to bruises, broken bones, or the loss of a significant settlement as the result of your spouse's very thorough lawyer inserting a clause related to your use of such divorce-inducing language in your prenuptial agreement.

v. Excommunication. This contract expressly forbids the reader from making any comments of a hostile nature toward religious officials or deities of any kind, since that could result in your eternal damnation; should you disregard this advice and be sent to hell, Lady Snark will not put in a good word for you with the management.

4. Indemnification

The reader agrees to indemnify, defend, and hold harmless Lady Snark for anything bad that happens to a third party as a result of your reading this book and/or acting misguidedly upon the contents thereof. For example, if you were to hide a Gila monster in your malevolent great-grandmother's coat closet at Christmas because you really needed that inheritance for a mint condition set of Astro Boy action figures, which have only just become available online, and then your cousin's girlfriend Polly was the one to get bitten and die instead because she couldn't stand your great-grandmother either and wanted to leave early, you are on the hook, not Lady Snark. Not only that, but if Polly's family decided to sue Lady Snark, you would be obliged to tell everyone in court that it was your own dumb idea.

5. Third Party Rights

If something wretched is enacted upon you by someone who has read this book, don't come running to Lady Snark (see Clause 4, Indemnification, above). But while we are on the subject of third parties, you realize that loaning your copy of this book to a third party could put your life in peril, particularly if you are wealthy and have promised to leave that very person your house or other valuables upon the shuffling off of your mortal coil. It would be better in any case for your friend to buy their own copy as this would also be more beneficial to Lady Snark's bank account.

6. Severability

If the reader is fragile in nature and his or her limbs are easily severed, that reader is advised even more than other people to utterly and completely avoid following any of the advice presented in this book; if you ignore this and find that the victim of your cruel slights retaliates with violence, not only is Lady Snark not responsible for your medical expenses, but you will also almost certainly regret the loss of your appendages.

7. Unauthorized Use

This book should not be used for anything but its explicitly stated goal, which is to help Lady Snark overcome her financial difficulties. It should not be used, for example, to write blackmail notes on; as a flammable material in committing arson; or any other use not stated directly by Lady Snark. In particular, it should most certainly not be employed as a coaster for cold drinks on the patio.

8. Miscellaneous

Don't poke yourself in the eye with a stick.

Acknowledgments

This book would not have been possible without the help of my charming agent, Ted Weinstein. Nor would this book or Lady Snark have been quite the same without the useful feedback of my editor, Jennifer Kushnier, or my principal readers: Michele Cauch, Heather Stephenson, Lorna Des Roses, Tim Kemp, and Haidee Lorrey. For their cheerleading of my writing aspirations over the years, I am grateful to Floyd and Lori Kemp, Ratsy, Amy Yamasaki, Fergal Jackson, David Wolfson, Josh White, Rema Iyer, Natalia Walter, Eppie Boze, Charles Coe, Hiroe Nakajima, and Professor Charles Meyer.

I also thank my many friends, supporters, and caffeine suppliers at the Diesel Café in Somerville, MA, and the 1369 Coffeehouse in Cambridge, where this book was written. The conversational distractions of John Corcoran, Liz Loveland, Alan Wiswall, Nick Gross, Lisa Nold, Reggie Franklin, and many others too numerous to mention were invaluable to my sanity. Thanks also to everyone at the National Writers Union for their support and advice. Finally, I'd like to acknowledge the talented Rachel McPherson, who volunteered to take Lady Snark's portrait, despite the fact that Rachel had met her briefly at a dinner party and knew what she was like.

About the Authors

Linguist and pop culture maven A. C. Kemp is the director of the award-winning American slang Web site *www.slangcity.com*, and her innovative classes on slang and American culture have been profiled in *The Boston Globe* and *The Christian Science Monitor*. She is a lecturer in Foreign Languages and Literatures at the Massachusetts Institute of Technology.

Etiquette expert Lady Snark grew to fame through her deportment class for inmates at the Haverford Women's Correctional Facility. Once a world traveler, the much-widowed and twice-incarcerated authoress now lives year round in Bar Harbor, as the conditions of her parole prevent her from leaving the excruciatingly dull state of Maine. You can learn more about the countess on her Web site, *www.ladysnark .com*.